WEIGHT TRAINING FOR THE OVER-35s

WEIGHT TRAINING FOR THE OVER-35s

Mary Southall and E. G. Bartlett

David & Charles
Newton Abbot   London   North Pomfret (Vt)

Acknowledgement

The authors gratefully acknowledge the advice and help given in the preparation of this book by Lynda C. Spear, IHBC (International Health and Beauty Credits), FETC (Further Education Teacher's Certificate Credit), WFBB (Welsh Federation of Body Builders), Miss Wales 1982 and 1983.

British Library Cataloguing in Publication Data

Southall, Mary
    Weight training for the over-35s
    1. Weight lifting
    I. Title   II. Bartlett, E. G.
    796.4′1   GV546.5

    ISBN 0-7153-8957-2

Line illustrations by Jennifer Johnson

Phototypeset by Typesetters (Birmingham) Ltd
Smethwick, West Midlands
and printed in Great Britain
by Redwood Burn Ltd, Trowbridge
for David & Charles Publishers plc
Brunel House   Newton Abbot   Devon

Published in the United States of America
by David & Charles Inc
North Pomfret   Vermont 05053   USA

Contents

Introduction

Men and women over thirty-five who take up weight training will have a different purpose in so doing from younger people, and whilst the exercises will be much the same, the approach and the schedules must reflect the different purpose.

Young people take up weight training for a variety of reasons. Often they want simply to develop their physiques or to correct faults in their development; sometimes they want to prepare for weight lifting contests and sometimes they use weight training to help their performance in other sports. In the spheres of body-building and weight-lifting there are local, regional, national and international contests, bringing a competitive element into these forms of training. But whilst competitions at all levels occasionally include a category for the 'over-35s', and holiday centres run 'fun' contests for older people, in general those who enter will be those who are simply continuing what they have already been doing for some years; they will not be people who have started after the age of thirty-five.

Newcomers to any sport who are over the age of thirty-five will have one or more of the following purposes:
- They will want to keep fit
- They will want to slow down the aging process
- They will want to correct weaknesses
- They will want to deal with the specific ills of age.

The particular value of weight training in helping these purposes is that its effect is all round. Other sports tend to develop the particular muscle groups involved. Thus jogging is good for stamina, breathing and the legs, but what about the arms, trunk and neck?

Weight training differs from weight-lifting, and it is important at the outset to understand that difference. Weight training is using weights to develop muscles or to keep in trim. Weight-lifting involves picking up the heaviest load one can in a recognised competition lift. The latter is not a sport to be contemplated by older people, unless they have been doing it all their lives.

Older people must, of course, approach training with caution. It is of no use buying a set of weights in the nearest sports shop and rushing home to do all the exercises suggested. That would result in strain or hernia or, at the very least, such stiffness and discomfort that the weights would be thrown to one side before being given a fair trial. The over thirty-fives, particularly if they have not been physically active for some years, must break themselves in gently, using free-standing exercises without weights for the first six to eight weeks, and only gradually coming to the use of weights. Indeed, it would be wise for those who have hitherto led a very inactive life or suffered from recent illness to consult a doctor before embarking on weight training.

There is no need to buy weights at all today; leisure centres provide machines on which to train and these allow the same muscle groups to be exercised working against resistance. We will look at the relative advantages of working at home or in a leisure centre later in this book.

First, it is necessary to consider the aging process and the specific dangers to fitness with advancing years; then the different apparatus available for training at home and in leisure centres should be looked at together with the basic principles of training. The preparatory course uses no weights but fits the body for the heavier work to come. The full training programme covered by this book will bring you to a peak fitness for your age group, and then you can add specific exercises for special muscle groups. Chapter 9 shows how other sports can help, and how weight training can help in sports performance. There are free-standing exercises that can be performed at odd moments to maintain suppleness and ward off encroaching age, and it is necessary to consider diet, general rules of health, the psychological approach to training, coping with stress, and weight control.

In all programmes using weights, mention will be made of training at home with dumb-bells only, or with bar- and dumb-bells, and training at leisure centres with the apparatus available there.

Do not be put off by thinking that you are too old. Certainly no one over thirty-five can expect miracles. The skeletal structure is fully developed by the age of twenty-six, and after that age you can only build on what you have. But you can correct faults, and achieve a greater degree of fitness; you can slow down the aging process and ensure a more satisfactory quality of life. In weight training there are no losers, because as soon as you pick up a dumb-bell, you are taking the first step to personal improvement. Men and women alike may benefit, and neither sex nor age should be considered a barrier.

1 The Aging Process in Men and Women

Although average life expectancy has increased in the last hundred years from just below fifty to well over sixty for men, and from under fifty to over seventy for women, it is now levelling out, and the Biblical norm of three score years and ten is a reasonable expectation for the healthy man or woman. If both your parents were long-lived, you could expect to go on into the eighties, and the reason the average figure is so much lower is because many people die much younger, either through illness or accident. If you can get through the childhood ailments without succumbing and then avoid accidents, you have a good chance of reaching old age. This means that the healthy thirty-five-year-old can expect another thirty-five years at least.

But it is not just the years that are left that must be considered; it is the quality of life, and that will depend in very large measure upon good health, to which exercise, of course, contributes so much. This chapter will try to identify the particular ills of aging then see what can be done about them.

A national health survey carried out in the United States for the years 1960 to 1970 put three illnesses at the top of the list of those attacking older people: heart conditions, arthritis and rheumatism. These three complaints were found to affect 10% of the population under forty-five, but the figure rose to more than 40% for those aged sixty-five or over. These complaints can be helped by exercise, watching your weight and avoiding stress. A high proportion of deaths amongst managerial staff was due to cirrhosis of the liver; cutting down on alcohol would decrease the risk.

At thirty-five most people feel in their prime. They have probably reached their professional goals; the mortgage is being paid off; the family is growing up; and whilst they still have to work hard, they begin to feel they can coast along without the frenzied drive thought essential to success in their early twenties. It is possible to relax and there is no reason not to do so. Indeed, as may be seen in Chapter 14, there are positive advantages in reducing pressure and pace. But while doing this, it is important not to reduce participation in exercise or indulge the appetite too much. Too often during these middle years people withdraw from active participation in sport, and at the same time, with success has come an easier life style, a car to take them where they formerly walked, labour-saving devices to do the work and expense account lunches to pamper their stomachs.

A good honest look at the dangers ahead may be just what is needed at this stage to persuade people to take regular and systematic exercise. Just as property is insured against damage, so bodies need to be insured against ill-health. Here are the special dangers:

Heart Disease
Heart troubles account for one third of the deaths in the Western world. Most of these are due to coronary artery disease or hypertension. Coronary artery disease is caused by atherosclerosis, which is a narrowing and hardening of the arteries by a build-up of fat. This fatty tissue, called atheroma, restricts the flow of blood, diminishes the elasticity of the artery and erodes the wall. You may not notice any symptom for years, and then experience only cramps after exercise which may well be dismissed without the true significance being recognised.

Eventually, however, if you neglect these early signs, you may suffer angina or a heart attack, or perhaps a stroke, if blood is not reaching the brain.

Men and women over thirty-five are at greater risk, and smoking, high blood pressure or eating foods rich in cholesterol will increase that risk. What can you do? There are three things:

- **Reduce your intake of animal fats and dairy produce.** Chapter 11 will help you plan a suitable diet.
- **If overweight, reduce.** Chapter 12 will help here.
- Most important of all, **take regular planned exercise but do not overdo it.** Read on, first.

Arthritis and Rheumatism

These are common, non-medical terms, that cover a number of painful conditions. Osteo arthritis is pain in the joints due simply to wear and tear. It usually affects the hip, knees or spine, and affects nine out of ten people over the age of forty, but is not generally considered serious. The main steps you can take are to reduce if overweight and so take some of the workload off the joint, and to strengthen the muscles by exercise. Keeping warm relieves the pain temporarily. Rheumatoid arthritis is a long-term disease of the joints, in which the synovial membrane becomes inflamed and swollen, leading to inflammation in other parts of the joint. Usually it is the knuckles, toes and wrists that are affected, but knees, ankles and neck can also suffer. About one person in two hundred suffers, and a doctor should be consulted, but moderate exercise, particularly swimming in a heated pool, helps.

Respiratory Diseases

The most frequent of these is the common cold, and little can be done about that, although, oddly enough, immunity is developed with age, and bronchitis is more likely to affect older people. Men are at greater risk than women. Air pollution and a damp atmosphere are contributory factors, and those who have weak lungs are the most susceptible. Bronchitis always requires medical treatment, but exercising the lungs in youth will reduce liability to the complaint in later years. Asthma is another common respiratory complaint, but it generally starts in childhood and to experience a first attack in middle age is rare. It is sometimes related to stress or allergies or emotional upsets or even exercise, and those suffering from asthma must consult a doctor before embarking on a course of exercises.

Cancer

Cancer accounts for the death of one in four people over the age of thirty-five. It is not a single disease but a group of diseases in which body cells multiply and spread uncontrollably. Many cases can be treated successfully if detected early. It is believed that 80% of cases result from environmental contamination. Additives in food should be avoided, animal fats eaten sparingly, smoking given up and alcohol restricted. The healthy diets in Chapter 11 should be studied.

Diabetes Mellitus

This is caused by a deficiency or total lack of insulin production by the pancreas. It becomes an increasingly common condition with age, and it is worth noting that being overweight is a contributory factor.

Stress

This is not an illness in itself, but it gives rise to many illnesses. It is dealt with fully in Chapter 14, as it is most likely to affect people in the older age groups.

Back Trouble

This condition is said to be responsible for more lost working hours than any other cause in Britain. Often there seems little doctors can do about it, although chiropractors and osteopaths claim a high success rate in treating patients. Exercise will strengthen the muscles and reduce the risk, and correct posture (Chapter 15) will alleviate the trouble. As bad posture also affects the lungs, it is worth paying attention to this detail.

Menopause

The menopause cannot be considered an illness as it is a natural feature of aging, but it does cause problems for a lot of women, and men are not without some manifestation of the changes either.

The menopausal years are approached nowadays with quite different attitudes from those of our parents or grandparents. Women have new understanding of their bodies and know that severe symptoms can be treated. The first thing to realise is that it does not last for ever, and that you will come out of this phase happier and more mature, and often far healthier and more energetic than you were before. Then you will find fresh pleasure in sexual relationships, because they will be free from the fear of unwanted pregnancy and the necessity for contraception.

Menstrual periods usually stop between the ages of forty-five and fifty-three. After this, the ovaries cease to produce a monthly egg, and the levels of the hormones oestrogen and progesterone fall. The build-up to the menopause takes several years, and the effects vary greatly in intensity and duration. Some women calmly sail through with no problem, though about three-quarters experience some symptoms.

Many women experience extreme mood swings, depressed one minute and full of elation the next. If depression lasts for a long time, they become unhappy, and aches and pains occur which aggravate the depression. The answer lies in relaxing, and in accepting these feelings as the normal and temporary effects of the menopause. Panic does not help.

The commonest symptoms complained of are hot flushes, which can vary from a warm feeling to blushing a fiery red and finding oneself soaked in perspiration. The cause of these flushes is metabolic, due to the hormone imbalance, which causes blood to rush into the surface blood vessels, giving a sudden feeling of extra heat, which the perspiration cools down. They will stop spontaneously after a while and the best way to cope is to say cheerfully, 'that's another one nearer the last'.

Physical alterations take place at the menopause in the reproductive organs, and most women are not aware of what is happening. Breasts sometimes decrease in size and are less firm. Vaginitis may occur when the lining of the vagina becomes thinner and more vulnerable to infection. This can lead to itching, dryness and painful intercourse.

These conditions can all be helped by medical attention. The important thing is to seek help in good time. There are Well Women Clinics and community groups which meet to give advice and support. Known treatments are better than trying to dose yourself or suffering silently. If the effects of the menopause are severe, Hormone Replacement Therapy (HRT) can be given and, under strict medical supervision, the risks of this treatment are minimal.

Talk to your husband and family and explain to them how you feel. Relax, and let others take care of you. Try early nights with good books. Carry on your normal life as far as possible. Keep in shape by regular exercise. Eat correctly and watch your weight, as recommended later in this book, and remember that weight increase is not inevitable at this time, though more careful monitoring is necessary until your metabolism settles down.

Many women report that after the menopause, they feel sexier than they ever did when they were younger, so you have something to look forward to.

The male menopause has not received quite so much attention because the changes and discomforts are not so obvious, but a man may find that his sexual drive diminishes and his pleasure in sex takes a dip. Some men do not seem to mind; some see it as a challenge; others seek younger women to rejuvenate their urges. The latter course is the worst of the options.

Seek new interests and friends. Exercise regularly. Watch your weight. These are the things that can give life back its sparkle, and enable you to enjoy a full sex life into old age.

Miscellaneous Illnesses

Illnesses most frequently associated with aging are loss of sight or hearing, which can usually be corrected by glasses or a hearing aid; indigestion, which can lead to worse troubles such as hernia, appendicitis, ulcers etc, all of which require medical attention;

bladder and prostate troubles, which are common in older men; varicose veins, due to standing still too long; loss of sexual powers in the male; the menopause in the female. Attention to general health through diet and exercise reduces the risks and makes us more fit to receive treatment when we do become affected.

Skin, Bone and Muscle Renewal

All cells in the human body are renewed every seven years, but there is a deterioration in skin, muscles and bones with increasing age. Wasting of muscle under the skin leads to wrinkles; poor circulation leads to the pallor of old people; muscles waste because of inactivity. Regular exercise becomes essential. As people grow older, they tend to absorb less calcium; this leads to brittle bones and deterioration of the teeth. Sitting about or prolonged bedrest after illness can increase the loss of calcium. The deficiency cannot be reversed by taking calcium tablets nor by the hormone treatment that is sometimes tried. The only thing that will overcome it is regular exercise combined with correct diet.

Accidents

The elderly have always been more accident prone. Speed of reaction, loss of sight or hearing, and lack of awareness are all contributory factors. Exercise helps to maintain alertness and will cut the risk of accidents. It has been found, for example, that, to avoid a car, a boxer walking in the roadway will jump back onto the pavement more quickly than an ordinary man. His training enables him to cut a few seconds off his reaction time, and this may well save his life in an emergency. It is not necessary to take up boxing to develop this advantage, of course; any exercise will help because exercise improves physical and mental co-ordination.

From this brief survey of the aging process, it can be seen that the dangers increase with the years and, of course, it is impossible completely to eradicate the natural process. Nor should that be done since old age and death are natural phenomena. It is important, though, to maintain bodies and minds in the best health possible, since this will increase a person's quality of life.

Many ills and conditions mentioned can be avoided by exercise and diet. Those which do not respond directly can certainly be helped by the fitness that exercise brings. Bearing in mind the provisos of Chapter 5, you can take up exercise at any time, but the sooner you start, the better.

Be positive. Start today. Get healthy and stay healthy, and you will enjoy life so much more.

2 Basic Principles of Weight Training

Weight training provides all round exercise. It should never be thought of as a way of building up one group of muscles only, but always as a way of maintaining or developing the physique as a balanced whole. It is true, of course, that if you detect any specific areas of under-development, you can specialise in them as part of your programme, but this specialisation must be part of a balanced programme, or strains to other muscles may result.

This chapter will answer some of your basic questions about weight training.

How Does It Work?

The body grows naturally from infancy until the age of twenty-one or twenty-two, and progress during this time depends on environmental and hereditary factors. Full natural development is reached in the early twenties, and the bone structure is set by the age of twenty-six. You must accept that your skeletal structure at that age is all you will ever have, and the only improvement you can make is by developing muscles and improving your posture. These efforts can transform your appearance, however.

The earlier you begin a development programme the better; indeed, it is usually young people in their late teens or early twenties who are most conscious of their physical defects and who take up weight training to improve. By the age of thirty-five that stage of development has passed. It is still possible to build muscle but it will take a little longer, and the main aim at that age is to maintain physique and not to allow it to deteriorate.

Building muscle depends on a simple principle. Exercise breaks down tissue, but Nature rebuilds and to make sure builds a little more than you have broken down. When next you exercise and break down tissue, Nature again builds that extra. So the muscle grows. Of course, this growth depends on adequate rest for the rebuilding to take place, and on the right intake of food. Protein is particularly needed.

If therefore you aim to develop a muscle, you must proceed in each exercise to the point where you just cannot manage another repetition, so that you are using the muscle to its limit, and then you must try to extend that limit. This point is called 'the point of resistance'. That final repetition is the important part. Then you must allow a forty-eight hour rest period for rebuilding.

If, however, you just want to maintain your physique, you need only see that each muscle gets adequate work to do; you need not proceed to the point of resistance. Enough exercise to make you pleasantly tired is sufficient.

If you want to slim, you should think in terms of doing a large number of repetitions of every exercise so that you burn up energy, but you must avoid using heavy weights, since this would build up muscle. All these techniques will be considered in the appropriate places.

Years ago, when weight training was less scientific, everyone used the same exercise charts, regardless of size and body structure. Today we know that training must be related to body type. Are you big-boned, solid and bulky? You are an endomorph. Are you small-boned, thin and energetic? You are an ectomorph. Are you in between, the well-muscled athletic type? You are a mesomorph.

You must relate training to your body type. In general this means that the big man will use lighter weights with higher repetitions. This is the exact opposite of what you might expect, and what people would prefer. The big man would like to do fewer repetitions with a heavier weight, since he could easily handle it; the smaller man is usually energetic and would like to use the lighter weight and to do more repetitions. To achieve results, each must stick to the training appropriate for his or her type.

When Should You Train?

It is best not to train within an hour and a half of a meal, and you should allow a period of relaxation after training before you go to bed. Working men and women will probably find the evenings the most convenient. Housewives and those whose working hours are flexible may find the mornings better, particularly if training at a leisure centre, as it might be easier to book the facilities at that time.

How Often Should You Train?

To keep healthy as in Chapters 5, 6 and 7, or to develop specific muscle groups as in Chapter 8, three sessions a week are needed. Monday, Wednesday and Friday, or Tuesday, Thursday and Saturday, but not both. For helping other sports as in Chapter 9, twice a week is adequate. For Slimming, as in Chapter 12, or for Slowing Down the Aging Process as in Chapter 10, it will not hurt to train every day, but do not over-exhaust yourself.

Where Should You Train?

In a room that is warm but not hot and where there is plenty of fresh air. A room with a full length mirror, such as the bedroom, is useful since you will be able to watch yourself in the mirror. This not only ensures you are doing the exercise correctly, it also concentrates your attention on the muscle involved, and this has been found to assist development. If you go to a leisure centre or a commercial gym, these conditions will probably be met.

What Should You Wear?

Loose clothes and the minimum for comfort is the answer. Your body needs to breathe, not only through the nose but through the pores. Movements should be free and not hampered by restrictive garments. Men find shorts or trunks adequate. Women wear shorts or slacks and a T-shirt. Some leisure centres insist on a track suit for both sexes.

Be sure to wrap up warmly between exercises; do not chill off. Be sure to wear low heeled shoes when using weights or machines, otherwise you risk flat feet.

What Weight Should You Use?

If you are aiming to develop muscle as in Chapter 8, the formula is this: load the dumb-bell or barbell or set the machine resistance to a level where you can perform the exercise once only and that with some effort. Then for men, ectomorphs use 70%, mesomorphs 65% and endomorphs 60%. For women, ectomorphs use 60%, mesomorphs 55% and endomorphs 50%.

At one time women used the same weight as men, but experience has proved that better results are obtained if they use the lighter weight and do more repetitions.

If, however, you are following the general training programmes in Chapters 6 and 7, choose a weight or machine resistance that enables you to do ten repetitions in each set if a man and twelve if a woman.

How Can I Tell If I Need To Develop?

The tables below give reasonable development for a man and a woman. Take your own measurements and see how you compare. If you are dissatisfied, the programme in Chapters 6 or 7 combined with that in Chapter 8 will help you to improve.

Of course, these charts of measurements and weights must only be taken as broad guidelines, since human beings differ so much in structure and development. They relate to a person aged thirty-five. After that age, there is often a slight weight increase up to the age of fifty, as less energy is used up with increasing age. There is also a tendency to put on fat, around the middle in a man, and around the shoulders, upper arms and thighs in a woman. Child bearing will also alter a woman's figure.

To offset these developments, more exercise or less food, or a combination of both is needed. Later in life height is lost, often as much as 3in as old age approaches.

There is also a wastage of muscle. Again, these effects can be minimised by regular exercise.

Is There Anything Else To Consider?

Yes, total life style, which is dealt with in Chapter 15, and heartbeat.

Exercise raises the heartbeat rate. To maintain health, we need to raise it and become out of breath at least three times a week by activity other than sex; we must stay within safe limits however. The normal pulse rate is just over 70.

The safe limit for a beginner is, 220 −your age × 60%

For an athletic type used to exercise, 220 −your age × 70%

For an experienced weight trainer, 220 −your age × 80%

If training with barbell or dumb-bell, it is safer to have someone who can take the weight from you, in case of need. Weight lifters have these 'catchers' who take the weight, if they have picked up something too heavy.

	Male			Female		
	Small	Medium	Large	Small	Medium	Large
Height	5ft 7in	5ft 10in	6ft	5ft	5ft 4in	5ft 9in
Neck	14½in	16½in	17in	13in	14in	15in
Chest Normal	38in	42in	46in	34in	36in	39in
Expanded	40in	45in	49in	36in	38in	42in
Waist	28in	31in	34in	25in	26in	29in
Hips	32in	36in	38in	35in	37in	40in
Upper Arm Straight	11½in	13in	14½in	10in	11in	12in
Flexed	13½in	15in	16in	11½in	12½in	14in
Forearm	11in	12in	13½in	10in	10½in	11in
Wrist	6½in	7in	7½in	5½in	6in	6½in
Thigh	19in	21in	24½in	17in	18in	20in
Calf	13½in	14½in	16in	12in	13in	14in
Ankle	8in	8½in	9½in	6in	7in	8in

Height	Weight table, men			Height	Weight table, women		
	Small Build	Medium Build	Large Build		Small Build	Medium Build	Large Build
5ft	8st	8st 6lb	9st	5ft	7st 6lb	8st	8st 12lb
5ft 1in	8st 2lb	8st 8lb	9st 2lb	5ft 1in	7st 8lb	8st 4lb	9st 1lb
5ft 2in	8st 4lb	8st 10lb	9st 7lb	5ft 2in	7st 11lb	8st 8lb	9st 5lb
5ft 3in	8st 6lb	9st	9st 11lb	5ft 3in	8st	8st 12lb	9st 10lb
5ft 4in	8st 8lb	9st 2lb	10st	5ft 4in	8st 4lb	9st 2lb	9st 13lb
5ft 5in	8st 11lb	9st 5lb	10st 5lb	5ft 5in	8st 8lb	9st 4lb	10st 2lb
5ft 6in	9st 4lb	9st 10lb	10st 11lb	5ft 6in	8st 12lb	9st 9lb	10st 6lb
5ft 7in	9st 8lb	10st 2lb	11st 2lb	5ft 7in	9st 1lb	10st	10st 10lb
5ft 8in	9st 13lb	10st 5lb	11st 7lb	5ft 8in	9st 6lb	10st 4lb	11st
5ft 9in	10st 5lb	10st 11lb	11st 13lb	5ft 9in	9st 11lb	10st 8lb	11st 4lb
5ft 10in	10st 10lb	11st 1lb	12st 2lb	5ft 10in	10st 2lb	10st 11lb	11st 8lb
5ft 11in	11st	11st 6lb	12st 6lb	5ft 11in	10st 4lb	11st	11st 12lb
6ft	11st 6lb	11st 12lb	13st	6ft	10st 8lb	11st 4lb	12st 2lb

3 Apparatus

Before rushing into buying apparatus, consider first whether you want to train at home or in a leisure centre. Most local authorities have these centres now, and commercial gyms are springing up to cater for the current interest in weight training. There are various factors to consider before deciding to train in one of these establishments.

Centres and gyms are run in one of two ways. Either there is an instructor in charge and students follow the set course which he prescribes, though he may give private lessons as well as the class course; or the centre is open for all who pay the fee to go there and do their own thing. In the latter case, you need to know what you are doing.

The advantages of a centre or gym are that there is no initial outlay of capital. You can try the gym and if it does not suit you, you can go elsewhere or fall back on home training. The apparatus is modern and sophisticated and well outside the price range of the average citizen, even with room at home to set it up. Often saunas, jacuzzis and massage are part of the gym's package. You will also meet other enthusiasts there.

The disadvantages are: centres are often heavily booked; you might have to follow a course that does not exactly meet your needs; you might not be able to get in as often as you want, and you might find others using the apparatus you need to use next. On top of this, you might be the only older person training. You must consider also travelling time and the cost of transport.

Fees at leisure centres or gyms are in the region of £1 to £1.50 per night, though some offer special rates to older people at off-peak times. Your training will therefore cost about £3 per week, plus travelling expenses.

At this rate, for one year's fees, you could buy all the apparatus you need and train at home.

You would then enjoy privacy; you could follow your own individual course; you could arrange training times to suit yourself; and you might get your spouse to train too. If you want the sophisticated apparatus of a leisure centre without going to one, there are multi-gyms for home use, which incorporate most of the machines in one.

Look into the local leisure centre before deciding. You will find there that the machines are laid out around the room, each machine called a 'Station'. There are usually fifteen stations, and some gyms offer multi-gyms and loose weights on dumb-bells and barbells as well. By each station, you will find a notice describing its use. The normal method is to insert a pin at the resistance level you need to use. The weights themselves are on runners inside the machine and cannot fall out on you; the fifteen stations are:

1 **Leg Press Station** A padded seat with a back rest on a metal bar. It has resistance foot rests attached to an adjustable weight stack.
2 **Hip Flexor Station** A steel frame with a padded back, arm supports, and hand grips. It is fitted at a suitable height to allow floor clearance when you are supported on your forearms.
3 **Thigh and Knee Leg Extension Station** A padded bench with foot rollers connected to a weight stack.
4 **High Pulley Station** A curved bar with hand grips connected by cable to a high pulley and weight stack.
5 **Rowing Station** A weight stack attached

to low cables and stirrup handles. It has a padded seat and foot rests.

6 **Low Pulley Thigh Pulls Station** A foot strap and cable attached to a floor level pulley and weight stack.

7 **Dead Lift Station** An arrangement of weights on runners attached to the wall, with handles to raise.

8 **Abdominal Conditioner Station** A padded board adjustable to several angles, with foot rollers and hand grip.

9 **Chest Press Station** A padded bench or stool, with metal lifting arm and hand grips attached to a weight stack.

10 **Chest Bench Station** A seat with arm resistance pads at shoulder height, attached to a weight stack.

11 **Leg Squat Station** This consists of two shoulder pads attached to a lifting bar and weight stack.

12 **Dipping Station** A low metal support with rail and hand grips.

13 **Chinning Station** A high metal support with rail and hand grips.

14 **Standing Twister** A circular turntable platform attached to a handrail at shoulder height.

15 **Seated Twister** A circular turntable seat with a foot rest attached to a waist level handrail.

If you feel you would prefer to train at home, you can do so with a pair of dumb-bells. Chapter 6(i) gives a programme using dumb-bells only. If, however, you can add barbell, bench, and wrist roller, you can make your programme more interesting by varying your exercises as indicated in Chapter 6(ii). You will also find it easier to add suitable exercises from Chapters 8 and 9 to meet specific needs.

Dumb-bells and barbells are often sold as a set, and the cost is about £1 per one pound weight. Sets start at 60lbs and go up to several hundred pounds. It is best to start with a lower range and add more weights later. Be careful to buy standard sized bars, however, or you may be limited to going back to the same manufacturer for the extra discs. Second-hand sets are often advertised in body-building magazines and in *Exchange and Mart*, but if buying second-hand, make sure that the collars are not rusty and that they grip firmly when screwed down.

The following, in order of usefulness, is the apparatus you should buy for home training: Dumb-bells; these are sometimes of a fixed weight, but the more useful kind consist of a rod, which is a metal bar about a foot long; weights, which are discs with a hole in the middle to slip onto the rod; and collars, which are smaller discs that have a screw to tighten and hold the weights in place. The tightening screw can either be a peg or it can work with an Alan key. Dumb-bells with adjustable weight enable you to vary the load for different exercises or as your strength increases.

Next comes the bar, which is a rod 5 or 6 feet in length, equipped with collars like the dumb-bell rod to hold the disc weights in place. Collars are placed about nine inches from each end, weights slipped on, and outer collars put on to hold the weights firm. When loaded with weights the bar is known as a Barbell. When calculating the weight you are lifting, remember to take into account the fact that the bar itself probably weighs 7 or 8lb.

Then there is the bench, which can be an ordinary household bench about 18in high and long enough to support your head and body, with feet on the floor off one end. More elaborate padded ones of tubular steel are available in sports shops, as are adjustable ones, which enable the top to be set at various angles.

A wrist roller is another useful piece of equipment. This is a short wooden rod with a string attached to the middle. You attach a weight to the string and wind it up by turning the rod. You could make this apparatus yourself out of a piece of broomstick.

Additionally, for slimming (Chapter 12), you might consider getting an exercise bike or a rowing machine, but these are not essential for general training. The best plan is to start with the basic equipment and to build up as you feel the need for more.

In describing the use of apparatus, various terms are used with which you should become familiar:

Repetition The performance of an exercise

once only.

Set A number of repetitions.

Number of sets The number of times each set is to be performed allowing a minute's rest between each set.

Point of resistance The point in a set where you just cannot do one more.

Instructions are usually set out as '3 × 10' or 3 sets to the point of resistance.

The first means do 10, take a minute's rest, do 10 more, take a minute's rest, and then do the final 10.

The second means that in each set you carry on until you just cannot do one more, taking the minute's rest between sets. Thus you might find that you could manage 12 in the first set, 10 in the second, but only 7 or 8 in the third.

4 Muscles of the Body

The human body consists of a skeleton, which has 206 bones, supporting just over 600 muscles. Muscles are bundles of closely interlocking fibres; they are usually attached to bones, either directly or by tendons, which are tough inelastic fibres. There are three kinds of muscle: voluntary, involuntary and cardiac. The only ones that can be consciously developed are the voluntary ones, though exercise will indirectly benefit the others.

Women do not differ from men in the number of voluntary muscles they have, though of course there are anatomical differences and their bones are usually smaller. They have different strengths and weaknesses, too, and in particular should be wary of overhead lifting until they have first strengthened their back muscles with gentle exercise.

In any exercise programme, it helps to be able to identify the muscle being used and to know the purpose of that muscle. Weight trainers usually watch their movements in a mirror, and in body building this has a special advantage, as it seems possible almost to will a muscle to grow by concentrating upon it. This concentration is not so essential in a simple keep-fit programme.

Stand stripped in front of a mirror, and try to identify all your muscles with the aid of Diagrams A and B. If you are inclined to be fat, they may not be sufficiently clearly defined, but this will encourage you to lose the flab so that you can see them.

The muscles you should see are:

Sterno mastoids The muscles at the sides of the neck. They turn the head from side to side or lift it up and down.

Trapezius This muscle covers the shoulders and the upper part of the back of your neck. It turns the head and helps in any arm movement.

Deltoids The bands of muscles covering the shoulder joints. They raise the arms sideways or forwards.

Biceps The muscles at the front of the upper arm. They bend the arms.

Triceps The muscles at the back of the upper arm. They straighten the arms.

Pectorals The big triangular muscles at the front of the chest. They pull the arms in towards the body or push away.

Serratus magnus The little ridges of muscle under the armpits. They lift the arms sideways.

Supinator longus The muscle at the side and back of the forearm. It turns the wrist from side to side.

Flexors (of the forearm) The muscles at the front of the forearm. They bend the wrist inwards.

External oblique abdominals These muscles extend down the sides of the body from the lower ribs. They turn the body and bend it from side to side.

Abdominals (upper and lower) These run from the lower ribs to the pubic bone in front of the body. They bend the body forwards and lift the legs in front of the body.

Pectineus and adductor longus The muscles on the inside of the upper thigh which move the thigh inwards.

Rectus femoris The long muscle running down the front of the thigh. It raises the leg and straightens it.

Vastus internus The muscle at the side and back of the upper leg. It turns the leg.

Peroneus longus The muscle at the side of the lower leg. It helps turn the foot or rotate the leg.

Tibialis anticus The big muscle at the front of the calf. It bends the foot upwards.

Gastrocnemius and soleus These are at the side and back of the calf. The first bends the foot backwards; the main function of the second is to help you keep upright.

Infra spinatus and rhomboideus major These muscles (Diagram B) are at the back of the shoulder. They take the shoulders back and help any pulling movement.

Latissimus dorsi The large muscles at the back of the upper body. They turn the body and raise the arms.

Erector spinae The muscles in the small of the back. They straighten up the bent-over body.

Gluteus medius and gluteus maximus The fleshy muscles of the buttocks. They rotate and move the legs.

Vastus lateralis The muscle at the side and back of the upper leg. It bends the knee and raises the leg sideways.

Adductor magnus The muscle at the back of the inside of the upper leg. It turns the leg when pointing the foot outwards.

Biceps of the leg and semi-tendinosus These two muscles are at the back of the upper leg. They bend the leg backwards.

Tensor muscles and vastus externus The tensor muscle covers the hips; the vastus externus runs from it down the outside of the thigh. The muscles lift the leg sideways.

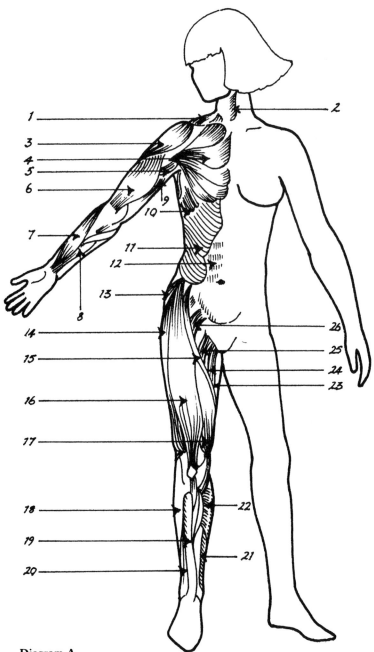

Diagram A

Anterior aspect

1 Trapezius	10 Serratus magnus	19 Tibialis anticus
2 Sterno cleido mastoid	11 External oblique	20 Peroneus brevis
3 Deltoid	12 Rectus abdominus	21 Soleus
4 Pectoralis major	13 Tensor	22 Gastrocnemius
5 Coraco brachialis	14 Vastus externus	23 Adductor magnus
6 Biceps	15 Sartorius	24 Gracillis
7 Supinator longus	16 Rectus femoris	25 Adductor longus
8 Flexors	17 Vastus internus	26 Pectineus
9 Triceps	18 Peroneus longus	

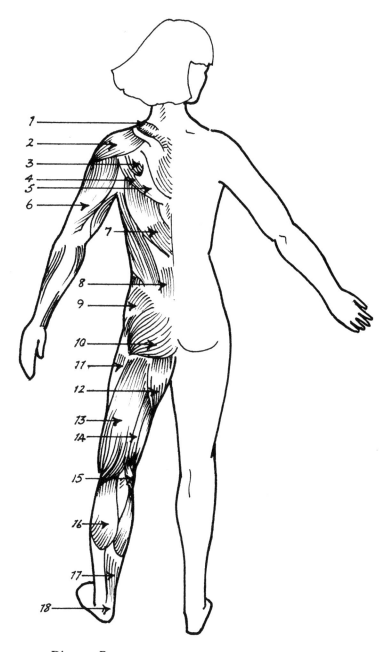

Diagram B
Posterior aspect

1 Trapezius
2 Deltoid
3 Infra spinatus
4 Teres major
5 Rhomboideus major
6 Triceps
7 Latissimus dorsi
8 Erector spinae
9 Gluteus medius
10 Gluteus maximus
11 Vastus lateralis
12 Adductor magnus
13 Biceps
14 Semi-tendinosus
15 Semi-membranosus
16 Gastrocnemius
17 Soleus
18 Tendo achillus

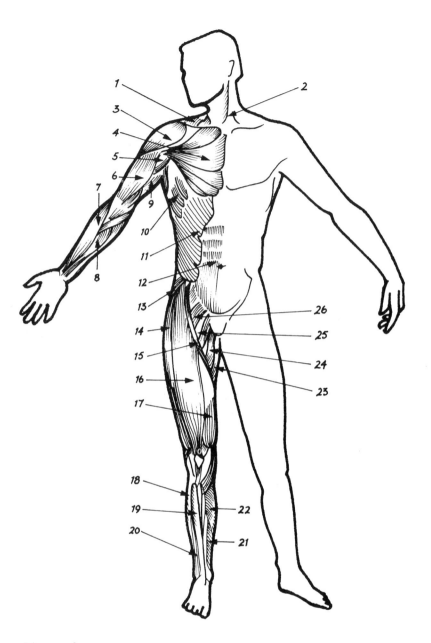

Diagram A

Anterior aspect

 1 Trapezius
 2 Sterno cleido mastoid
 3 Deltoid
 4 Pectoralis major
 5 Coraco brachialis
 6 Biceps
 7 Supinator longus
 8 Flexors
 9 Triceps
10 Serratus magnus
11 External oblique
12 Rectus abdominus
13 Tensor
14 Vastus externus
15 Sartorius
16 Rectus femoris
17 Vastus internus
18 Peroneus longus
19 Tibialis anticus
20 Peroneus brevis
21 Soleus
22 Gastrocnemius
23 Adductor magnus
24 Gracillis
25 Adductor longus
26 Pectineus

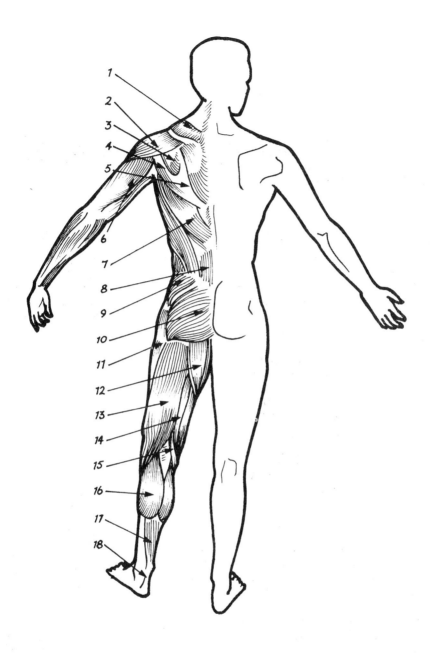

Diagram B

Posterior aspect

1	Trapezius	10	Gluteus maximus
2	Deltoid	11	Vastus lateralis
3	Infra spinatus	12	Adductor magnus
4	Teres major	13	Biceps
5	Rhomboideus major	14	Semi-tendinosus
6	Triceps	15	Semi-membranosus
7	Latissimus dorsi	16	Gastrocnemius
8	Erector spinae	17	Soleus
9	Gluteus medius	18	Tendo achillus

5 Introductory Free-standing Programme for Beginners

As mentioned in the Introduction, it is unwise to plunge into weight training without some preliminary exercise of a gentler nature first. This is particularly true for the older person, who may not have taken much part in physical sports since the age of twenty-five. The older you are, the more necessary to take care.

In this chapter is an introductory course that uses no weights at all; it will tone up the muscles and get the body in trim for the training ahead. Athletes or those who participate regularly in sport can omit this chapter and go straight on to weight training, but if in doubt, err on the side of caution, and work through this course first.

There are only ten exercises. Do them every other day and omit Sundays. Follow the course for six weeks.

Exercise 1 Knee Bends
Stand upright with feet normal distance apart, head erect and relaxed. Grasp the back of a chair with both hands, to maintain balance, and do the knees bend slowly and under control, going half-way down. If you cannot manage half-way to begin with go as far as you can, and aim to reach half-way with practice. Try not to lean forward.

In this as in all exercises breathing is most important. Breathe in as you go down, and out as you come up. The leg muscles benefit most, but the lungs are helped by the deep breathing.

Men and women do 2 × 10 for the first three weeks, then 3 × 10.

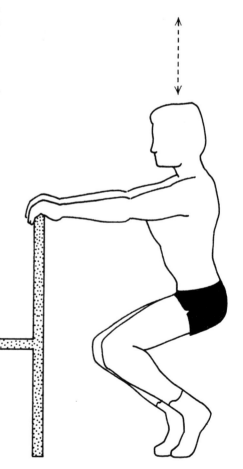

Fig 1

Exercise 2 Touching Floor Between Legs
Stand with feet astride, somewhat wider than normal stance. Take the arms above your head and back, breathing in deeply. Bend forwards smoothly and touch the floor or as far as you can go, between your legs, breathing out as you go down, and in as you come back up again. Do not force yourself with jerky movements, as the ability to reach the floor depends in part on the relative length of arms and legs. It has been found that forcing children to do this in school in years gone by has resulted in back troubles in later life, and bearing this in mind, the older person must take even greater care to avoid strain.

The muscles of the back and chest benefit.

Men and women do 2 × 10 for the first three weeks, then 3 × 10.

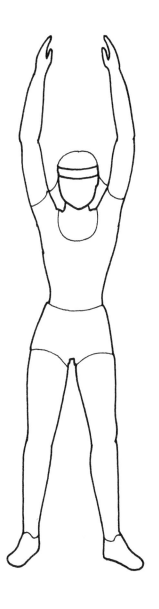
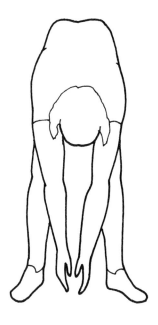

Fig 2 (a) and (b)

Exercise 3 Trunk Turning

Stand upright, feet a comfortable distance apart, arms stretched out sideways at shoulder level as far as possible. Try to keep your hips still and turn the trunk as far to the right as you can. Turn your head and look to your right rear and your body will follow. Your arms are kept in line with the shoulders. Come back to front and immediately turn to the left, continuing the movement rhythmically from side to side. Breathe freely.

The trunk muscles benefit.

Men and women do 15 each side for the first week, then add five each week.

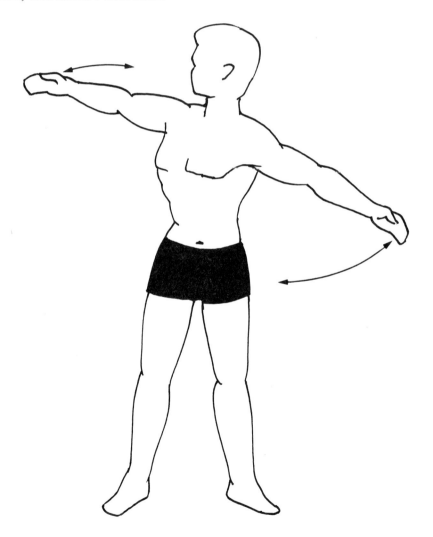

Fig 3

Exercise 4 Side Bends

Stand upright, feet together, hands at sides, and palms inwards. With your body facing front, bend as far over to the right as you can, letting the palm slide down the outside of your right leg. Reach as far down with your fingertips as possible. Straighten up and bend to the left in the same way. Breathe freely.

Muscles at the side of the body benefit.

Men and women do 15 each side for the first week, then add five per week.

Exercise 5 Head Circling

This one needs care. Do it very gently, and if necessary, support your neck by placing the hands on either side, though this is not essential and for the sake of clarity is not shown in the figure.

Stand upright, feet together. Bend your head forwards, as far as possible without straining, take it to your right shoulder, then up and back, then to your left, forward to the left shoulder, and to the centre again. After 5 circles in an anti-clockwise direction, reverse direction and do 5 clockwise. Breathe freely.

The neck muscles are strengthened.

Men and women do 5 each way throughout the course.

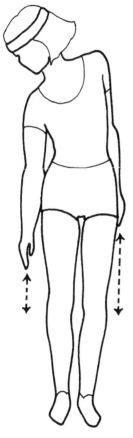

Fig 4

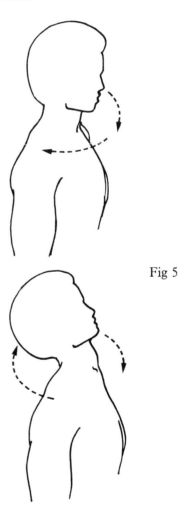

Fig 5

27

Exercise 6 Touching Alternate Toes

Stand with your feet wide apart, arms above head. Bend forwards, and with your right fingertips touch your left toes. Straighten up and then with the left fingertips touch your right toes. Continue alternating, breathing in as you come up and out as you go down. If you cannot quite get down to begin with, do not strain. Your performance will improve as you get more supple.

Hips, back and abdominal muscles all benefit, as do the arms by stretching and the chest by deep breathing.

Men and women do 2 × 10 for the first three weeks, then 3 × 10.

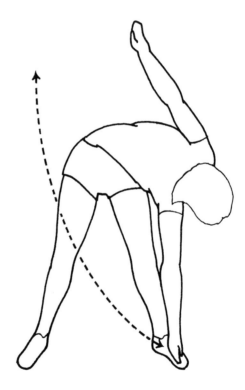

Fig 6

Exercise 7 Cobra to Cat Stretch

Take up the position in Fig 7(a), resting on your toes and the palms of your hands, back concave, head up, chest forwards. The position gets its name from the resemblance to a cobra rearing up. From this position, lower the head and arch the back to the position of Figure 7(b). A cat does this, which is why it is called the cat stretch. Support yourself on hands and toes throughout. Breathe in when in the first position and out as you arch your back.

Arms, shoulders, chest and back all benefit.

Men and women start with 10 only, increasing to 2 × 10 after three weeks.

Fig 7(a) and (b)

Exercise 8 Deep Breathing with Arms Swinging

Stand upright and relaxed, head up, shoulders back, feet normal distance apart. Cross the arms in front of you. Swing your arms upwards, sideways and backwards, breathing in deeply as you do so. Bring your arms back to the crossed position in front of you, breathing out.

Arms, chest, and posture all benefit.

Men and women do 10 only throughout the course.

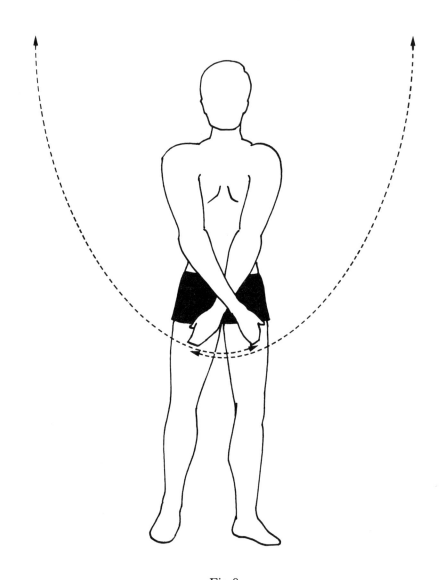

Fig 8

Exercise 9 Press Ups

Take up the position shown in Figure 9, resting your weight on your toes and on the palms of your hands turned inwards. Arms are straight, stomach in, head up. Breathe in as you lower your body by bending your arms, and out as you straighten your arms to press your body up to the starting position. Try to touch the floor with your nose, but if you cannot manage this at first, go as far down as you can, and try to go a little further each time.

Arm, shoulder, chest and abdominal muscles all benefit. In fact, this exercise combined with Exercise 1 will cover all the muscles of your body.

Men and women do one set of as many as they can manage for the first three weeks, then two sets of as many as they can manage.

Fig 9

Exercise 10 Relaxing

Stand upright. Let your arms hang loosely at your side. Shake each one gently in turn, letting the wrist relax as well. Think of your arm as a rope hanging from your shoulder joint, not stiff at all. Shake it gently, letting it sway for ten seconds. Do each arm in turn.

Then, raise one leg off the ground, and letting it hang loosely from your hip joint, gently shake that as well. Repeat with the other leg.

This exercise derives from karate training where it has been found useful in preparing the limbs for more strenuous movements.

Men and women do 10 seconds with each limb throughout the course.

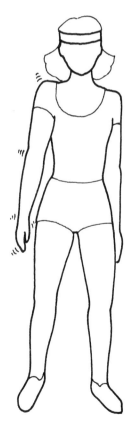

Fig 10

6 General Training Programme for Home Use

After conditioning your body with the Introductory Programme in the last chapter you are ready to start serious training with weights. The two programmes in this chapter are designed to bring your body to peak fitness, and to maintain it in that condition throughout your life. If you are looking for specific muscular development or for help with sports training, you will need to add some of the exercises from Chapters 8 or 9.

The first programme of 11 exercises makes use of dumb-bells only. The second programme uses mainly barbell.

This programme is intended for use at home, though it would be possible in a leisure centre if loose weights are available.

At the beginning of each weight training session, it is necessary to warm up with a few free-standing exercises and to cool down at the end. For these purposes use some of the exercises from the last chapter.

Follow this training programme every other night, omitting Sundays. Variations in exercises for men and women are shown where they occur. To warm up, do 10 each of **Exercises 1, 2, 3, 4, 5, 6 and 8.**

(i) Dumb-bell Programme

Exercise 11 Squats with Dumb-bells at Sides

Take a loaded dumb-bell in each hand and let them hang at your sides. Stand with your feet on a fixed plank about 1in off the ground, and with the dumb-bells hanging at your sides, do the Knee Bends as in Exercise 1, and come up again. Breathe in as you go down and out as you come up.

Legs, chest and arms all benefit.

Men do 2 × 10 increasing to 3 × 10 as they feel able. Women do 2 × 12 increasing to 3 × 12 as they feel able. If it becomes too easy, add a little weight.

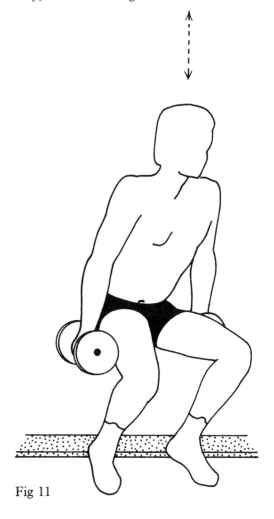

Fig 11

Exercise 12 Single Hand Dumb-bell Curls
Take a dumb-bell in the left hand, palm upwards. Let it hang down in front of you, back of hand touching your thigh. Bring the dumb-bell to your shoulder by bending your arm slowly. Breathe out as you bring it up, and in as you lower. Complete a set with your left hand, then repeat with the right. It helps to put your free hand behind you.

Biceps and triceps benefit.

Men do 2 × 10 increasing to 3 × 10. Women do 2 × 12 increasing to 3 × 12.

Exercise 13 Triceps Stretch Standing
Load the dumb-bell centrally, with a collar each side to hold the weights in position. Hold it in both hands above your head with knuckles to the front, palms to the rear. By bending your elbows, lower the dumb-bell behind your head, breathing in. Bring it back to the overhead position, breathing out. The upper arms remain vertical. Use a very light weight (2½lb) or even the bar on its own to begin with.

The exercise is for the triceps.

Men do 2 × 10 increasing to 3 × 10. Women do 2 × 12 increasing to 3 × 12. Add weight when it becomes too easy.

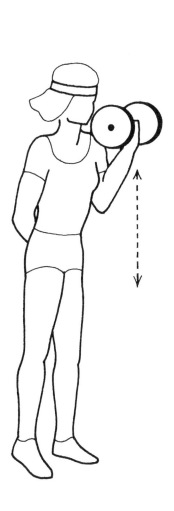

Fig 12

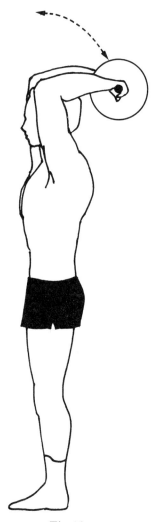

Fig 13

Exercise 14 Alternate Dumb-bell Presses
Take a loaded dumb-bell in each hand and bring them to rest on your shoulders. Straighten the right arm upward above your head and as you lower this to the shoulder, press the left one up. Breathe freely.

Arms and shoulders benefit.

Men do 2 × 10 increasing to 3 × 10. Women do 2 × 12 increasing to 3 × 12.

Exercise 15 Single Hand Rowing with Dumb-bell
Lean forwards from the waist and rest one hand on a table, bench or back of a chair. Take a dumb-bell in the other hand, palm towards your body, and let it hang down at arm's length. Bend your arm to bring it to shoulder level, breathing out as you do so, and lower again, breathing in. Stay in the bent-over position, and after doing a set with one hand, change hands and do a set with the other.

This exercise is for the latissimus dorsi.

Men do 2 × 10 increasing to 3 × 10. Women do 2 × 12 increasing to 3 × 12. Add weight as necessary.

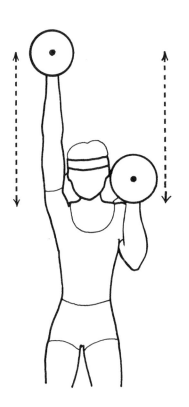

Fig 14

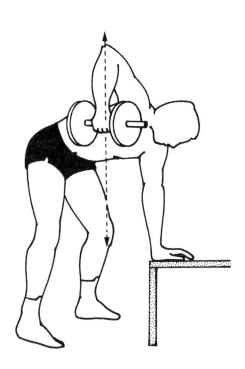

Fig 15

Exercise 16 Straight Arm Pullovers
For this, you need to lie on a bench, head at one end, feet on the floor at the other. Load the dumb-bell centrally, and hold it close to the centre, palms facing your body as it rests on your thighs. From this position, take it over your head and as far back as you can, with arms straight, breathing in. Bring it back to your thighs, breathing out.

The pectorals, shoulder muscles and rib-cage all benefit.

Men do 2 × 10 increasing to 3 × 10. Women do 2 × 12 increasing to 3 × 12. Add weight when necessary.

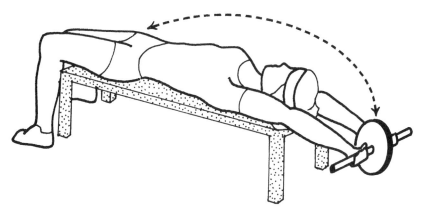

Fig 16

Exercise 17 Sit-ups
Lie flat on the floor, knees slightly bent, with your feet tucked under some object to prevent them coming up; a barbell is good if you have one, if not, heavy cushions will do. Clasp the hands at the back of the head. Now, sit up and bend forward as far as you can, pulling with the hands on the back of the head. Breathe out as you come up, in as you go down. Control the movement, and do not flop back.

The upper abdominals benefit.

Men do 2 × 10 increasing to 3 × 10. Women do 2 × 12 increasing to 3 × 12.

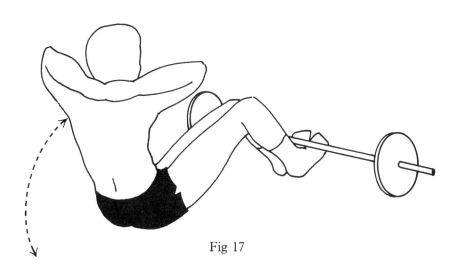

Fig 17

Exercise 18 Legs Raise from Prone Position

Lie flat on your back, arms at sides. Lift both heels off the floor. Raise each leg alternately, lowering one as you raise the other, but without putting the heels back on the ground until you come to the end of a set. Breathe freely.

The lower abdominals benefit.

Men do 2 × 10 with each leg increasing to 3 × 10. Women do 2 × 12 with each leg increasing to 3 × 12.

A variation of this exercise is to raise both legs together. This is slightly easier. If you do this, breathe out as you raise and in as you lower, and do twice as many in each set.

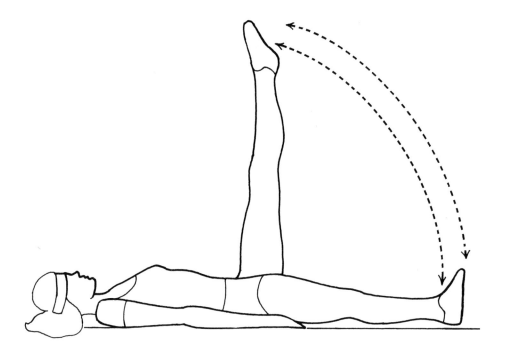

Fig 18

Exercise 19 Side Bends with Dumb-bells

Take a loaded dumb-bell in each hand using a very light weight or the bar only to begin with. Bend as far as you can to your left, letting the dumb-bell slide down the outside of your left leg, and curling the one in your right hand up under your armpit; then bend as far as you can to your right, letting the right arm slide down and the left curl up under the armpit. Breathe freely.

This exercise is for the external oblique abdominals and the tensors.

Men do 2 × 10 increasing to 3 × 10, each side. Women do 2 × 12 increasing to 3 × 12, each side.

Exercise 20 Trunk Turning with Dumb-bells

Take a dumb-bell in each hand and hold arms out in line with the shoulders. Feet are normal distance apart, body upright. Turn to your right as far as you can, taking the right arm back and the left forwards, to keep them in line with the shoulders. Try to keep the hips facing front and to turn from the waist. Come back to front facing and turn to the left. Continue turning from side to side rhythmically. Breathe freely.

The external oblique abdominals and the tensors benefit.

Men do 2 × 10 each side increasing to 3 × 10. Women do 2 × 12 increasing to 3 × 12 each side.

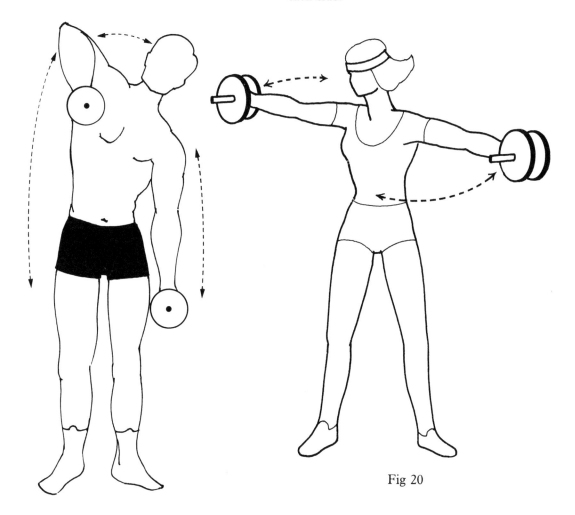

Fig 19

Fig 20

Exercise 21 Dumb-bell Raises

Stand with your feet a comfortable distance apart. Take a dumb-bell in your right hand, knuckles uppermost, and let it hang down at arm's length in front of you. Keep your other hand by your side. Raise the dumb-bell slowly forwards and upwards to shoulder level, keeping your arm straight, and breathing out. Lower slowly, breathing in. Do a set with the right hand, then change and do a set with the left.

Arm muscles and deltoids benefit.

Men do 2 × 10 increasing to 3 × 10 each hand. Women do 2 × 12 increasing to 3 × 12 each hand. Add weight when it becomes too easy.

To cool down, repeat **Exercises 8 and 10**. You may wonder why women are doing more repetitions. You must bear in mind that they will be using lighter weights, as indicated in Chapter 2.

(ii) Barbell Programme

Warm up with 10 each of **Exercises 1, 2, 3, 4, 5, 6 and 8.**

Exercise 22 Curls with Barbell

Stand with feet the normal distance apart. Take the barbell in both hands, shoulder-width apart, palms upwards, and let it hang at arm's length in front of you. From this position, bring the bar up to your chest by bending your elbows. Breathe out as you raise the bar, and in as you lower. Perform the movement slowly.

Biceps and triceps benefit.

Men do 2 × 10 increasing to 3 × 10. Women do 2 × 12 increasing to 3 × 12. Add weight when it becomes too easy.

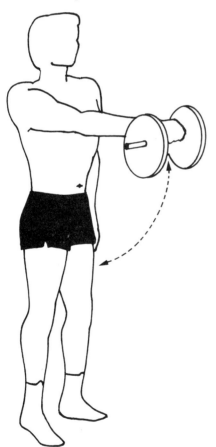

Fig 21

Fig 22

Exercise 23 Reverse Curls with Barbell
For this you need a very light weight, and may find it sufficient to use the bar alone. Hold the bar behind your body with both hands so that it rests across your buttocks or the top of your legs. Palms are to the front. Keeping the body upright, take the bar back as far as you can. This will only be a few inches, so do not lean forwards to make it more. Having reached that position, turn your wrists back so as to raise the bar another inch or so away from you. Return to normal with bar touching your body. Breathe out as you take the bar back, in as you return.

Triceps benefit.

Men do 2 × 10 increasing to 3 × 10. Women do 2 × 12 increasing to 3 × 12.

Exercise 24 Bent Over Rowing with Barbell
Stand upright, feet normal distance apart. Pick up the bar, hands shoulder-width apart, palms over the bar, thumbs under. Bend forwards until the body is at right angles to the ground. Keep the back flat and stay in the bent-over position throughout the exercise, arms hanging down. Bring the bar up to your chest by bending your elbows, breathing out. Lower to the hanging position, breathing in. Do not put the bar on the ground between repetitions.

Latissimus dorsi, triceps and biceps benefit.

Men do 2 × 10 increasing to 3 × 10. Women do 2 × 12 increasing to 3 × 12. Add weight when it becomes too easy.

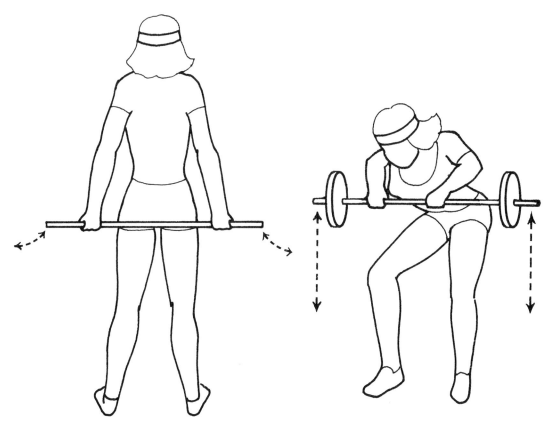

Fig 23   Fig 24

Exercise 25 Bench Press with Barbell

Lie on your back on a bench with the upper body, shoulders and head firmly supported, feet on the floor off one end. Take a wide grip on the bar, fingers over and thumb under, and let it rest high up your chest. With the bar in this position, take a deep breath, and push it straight upwards to arm's length, breathing out as you do so. Breathe in as you lower again.

Pectorals, biceps, triceps, front deltoids and the whole of the chest and back benefit.

Men do 2 × 10 increasing to 3 × 10. Women do 2 × 12 increasing to 3 × 12. Add weight when it becomes too easy.

Exercise 26 Knee Raises

Stand with your back to a wall, hands on hips. Raise your knees alternately, as high as you can towards your chest, keeping your body upright. Breathe out as you raise and in as you lower. Do the movement slowly and deliberately.

The leg muscles and the abdominals benefit.

Men do 2 × 10 increasing to 3 × 10. Women do 2 × 12 increasing to 3 × 12.

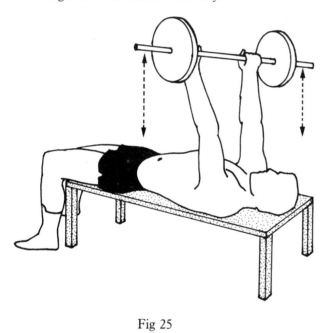

Fig 25

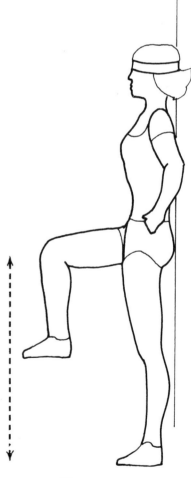

Fig 26

Exercise 27 Leg Raises on Bench
Lie on a bench, buttocks close to one end, so that your legs project beyond the bench. Take both legs up until they are level with the bench and horizontal. This is the starting position, and you must not put them on the ground until a set is complete.

From the starting position, raise the legs as high as possible, taking them over your head, and breathing out as you do so. Lower to the horizontal position, breathing in.

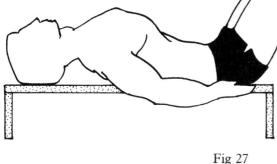

Fig 27

This is one of the strongest abdominal exercises known.

Men do 2 × 10 increasing to 3 × 10. Women do 2 × 12 increasing to 3 × 12.

Exercise 28 Side Bends with Dumb-bells
This is a repeat of Exercise 19. Use very light weights. The external oblique abdominals and the tensors benefit.

Men do 2 × 10 increasing to 3 × 10 each side. Women do 2 × 12 increasing to 3 × 12 each side.

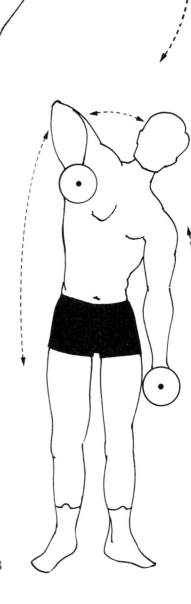

Fig 28

41

Exercise 29 Trunk Turning with Bar on Shoulders

Take the bar only onto the shoulders behind the neck as shown. You will need a wide grip, palms under the bar. Feet are a normal distance apart. From this position, turn from the waist as far to the right as possible, letting the head turn and the bar follow in line with the shoulders. Return to front facing and then turn to your left as far as possible. The object of the bar is to keep arms and shoulders in line.

Hips and muscles at the side of the body all benefit.

Men do 2 × 10 each side increasing to 3 × 10. Women do 2 × 12 each side increasing to 3 × 12.

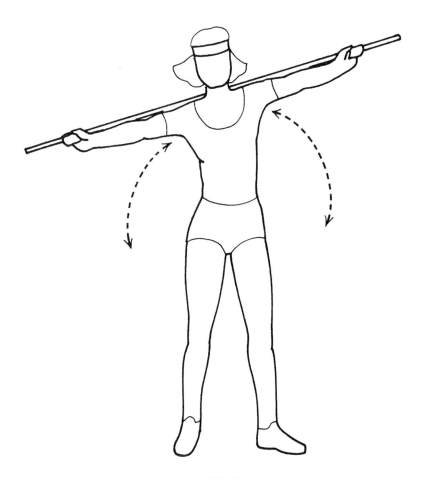

Fig 29

Exercise 30 Upright Rowing with Barbell
Stand upright, feet close together. Grip the bar with both hands close together near the centre. Make sure that it balances as you lift. Palms are facing your body. Let the bar hang down in front of your thighs. Take a deep breath, and as you breathe out, bring the bar up level with your shoulders, raising the elbows outwards. Try to make the bar touch your chin, and keep it as near your body as you can. Breathe in as you lower to the hanging position, and do not put the bar on the ground between repetitions.

The exercise is for the deltoids and trapezius.

Men do 2 × 10 increasing to 3 × 10. Women do 2 × 12 increasing to 3 × 12. Add weight when it becomes too easy.

To cool down, repeat **Exercises 8 and 10.**

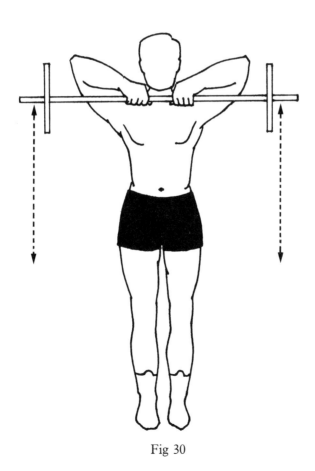

Fig 30

7 General Training Programme for Leisure Centre

Before starting this programme, work through the Introductory Free-standing Programme in Chapter 5. You will then be able to progress safely to a full training programme, using the machines at a leisure centre. The fifteen stations there are designed to provide an all-round work-out. Do fourteen on each visit, omitting the Standing Twister (Exercise 44) one week and the Seated Twister (Exercise 45) the next week, since these two stations exercise the same muscles.

As with the Home Programme in the last chapter, warm up with 10 each of **Exercises 1, 2, 3, 4, 5, 6** and **8**. Follow the training programme every other night, omitting Sundays.

Exercise 31 Leg Press
Sit with the back firmly against the seat, hands holding the seat rail. Breathe in. Press the feet firmly against the pedals, and extend the legs as far as possible, breathing out as you do so. Return to the starting position, keeping the tension on the weights.

Thigh and hip muscles benefit.

Men do 2 × 10 increasing to 3 × 10. Women do 2 × 12 increasing to 3 × 12. Increase the tension when required.

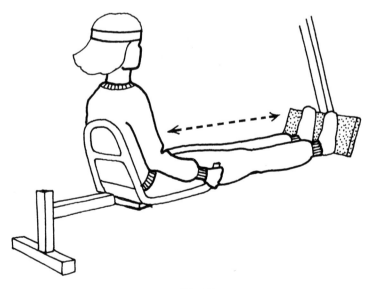

Fig 31

Exercise 32 Hip Flexor

Rest the arms on the forearm supports, and grasp the handgrips. Breathe in, and pull the knees to the chest as you breathe out. Roll your hips forwards to bring your knees as high as possible. Control the action all the way up and down, flexing the abdominals as much as possible. Breathe in as you lower your legs to the starting position.

Abdominals and hip muscles benefit.

Men and women do 2 sets of as many as they can manage, increasing to 3 sets.

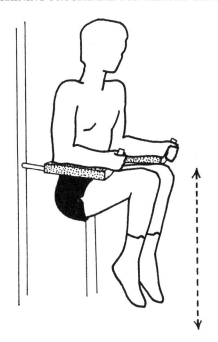

Fig 32

Exercise 33 Thigh and Knee Leg Extension

Sit on the machine and grasp the sides of the seat. Lock your ankles under the rollers; do not point the toes. Breathe in, and while you lift your legs to the full extension, breathe out. Flex your thighs and hold the extension for 1 second. Breathe in as you lower to the starting position.

Knee joints and leg muscles benefit.

Men do 2 × 10 increasing to 3 × 10. Women do 2 × 12 increasing to 3 × 12.

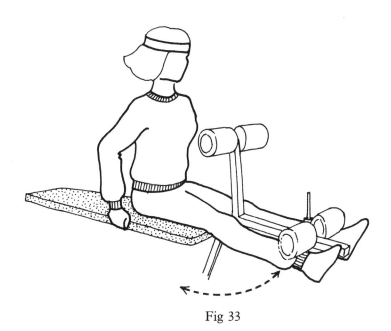

Fig 33

Exercise 34 High Pulley

Grasp the bar with a wide grip. Kneel on floor or sit on a low stool under the pulley. Keep your back straight. Breathe out as you pull the bar to either your chest or the back of your neck. Breathe in as you let the weights go back. Let the arms stretch to their complete extension. One week, pull to the chest; the next week pull to back of the neck.

Pectorals, latissimus dorsi, and arm muscles benefit.

Men do 2×10 increasing to 3×10. Women do 2×12 increasing to 3×12.

Exercise 35 Rowing

Sit upright, with soles of feet against the machine bar. Grip the handles, and pull elbows to shoulder level as you breathe out. Slowly release the tension as you breathe in, leaning forwards as the hands go back.

The deltoids, pectorals, trapezius, latissimus dorsi and abdominals all benefit.

Men do 2×10 increasing to 3×10. Women do 2×12 increasing to 3×12.

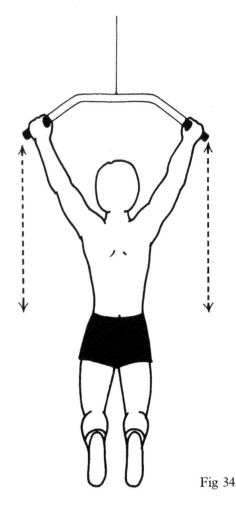

Fig 34

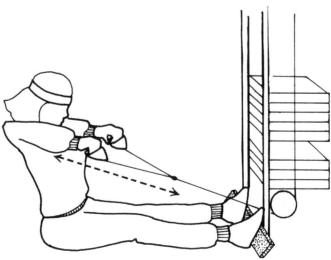

Fig 35

Exercise 36 Low Pulley Thigh Pulls

Stand with your right side to the machine, your left foot in the strap. Raise the left leg sideways as far as you can, breathing out. Breathe in as you return your leg to normal. Complete a set, then face the opposite way, still with the strap on your left foot. This time cross your left leg over your right, breathing out as you are crossing and in as you are lowering. Repeat the whole exercise with the strap on the other foot.

The first movement exercises the muscles on the outside of the leg; the second, the muscles on the inside of the leg.

Men do 2 × 10 increasing to 3 × 10. Women do 2 × 12 increasing to 3 × 12.

Exercise 37 Dead Lift

Stand upright facing the machine. Grasp the handles and pull upwards, raising the elbows outward and upward towards the ceiling. Breathe out as you raise the hands to your chin and in as you lower again.

The trapezius, deltoids, rhomboids and all the chest muscles benefit.

Men do 2 × 10 increasing to 3 × 10. Women do 2 × 12 increasing to 3 × 12. Add weight as you progress.

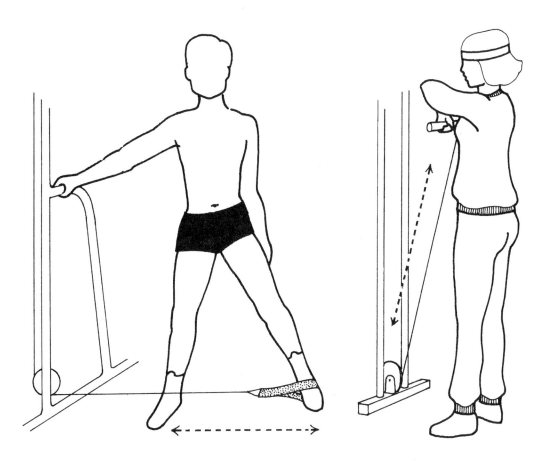

Fig 36   Fig 37

**Exercise 38 Abdominal Conditioner
Sit-Ups**

Sit on the board with your insteps under the rollers, knees bent. Clasp your hands behind your head. Sit up, and bring first your right elbow to your left knee and then your left elbow to your right knee. Breathe out as you come up, and in as you lower to the starting position.

Abdominal and hip flexor muscles benefit.

Men and women do 2 sets of as many as they can manage, increasing to 3 sets.

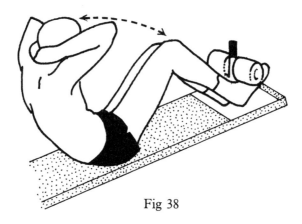

Fig 38

Exercise 39 Chest Press

Lie flat on the bench with feet on the floor. Grasp the handles, keep elbows close in to the body, and push handles upwards. Breathe out as you push up and in as you lower again.

Pectorals, triceps and deltoids benefit.

Men do 2 × 10 increasing to 3 × 10. Women do 2 × 12 increasing to 3 × 12. Add weight as needed.

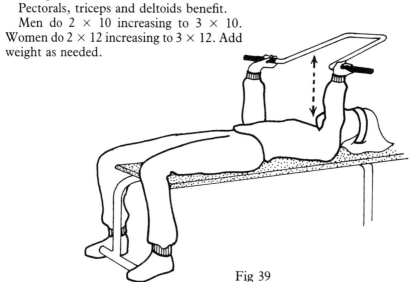

Fig 39

Exercise 40 Chest Bench
Sit on the seat, lift the arms and put them round the blocks to grip them in the most comfortable position. Keep head and back against the pads. Breathe in, and concentrate on forcing the elbows together as you breathe out. Breathe in again as you relax to the starting position.

Pectorals benefit in the main.

Men do 2 × 10 increasing to 3 × 10. Women do 2 × 12 increasing to 3 × 12.

Exercise 41 Leg Squat
Stand under the pads with knees bent, pads on shoulders. Grip the handles and straighten the knees against the resistance of the weight as you breathe out. Bend your knees as you breathe in.

Gluteus medius, gluteus maximus, erector spinae and abdominals all benefit.

Men do 2 × 10 increasing to 3 × 10. Women do 2 × 12 increasing to 3 × 12. Add weight as needed.

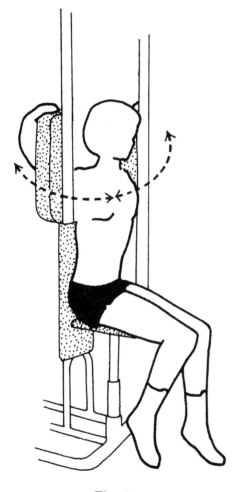

Fig 40

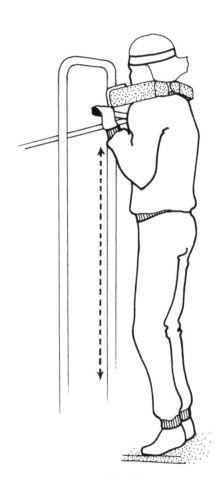

Fig 41

Exercise 42 Dipping

Place hands on hand grips. Breathe in, and as you breathe out, lift the body clear of the ground, until the arms are supporting you with elbows straight, then bend the knees at right angles. Now, dip your body between the supports, by bending the elbows, and come up again. Breathe in as you lower the body and out as you come up. If you cannot manage this exercise at first, lower yourself just a little, and progress until you are able to do the exercise fully.

Deltoids, pectorals and trapezius benefit.

Men and women do 2 sets of as many as they can manage increasing to 3 sets.

Exercise 43 Chinning

Place hands on hand grips. Breathe in, and as you breathe out, raise your body to bring your head above the bar, bending your elbows to do so. Hold the position a second before lowering back to the floor and breathing in. This is a very difficult exercise. Omit it if you find it impossible, but try if you can to raise yourself a little bit and you will improve with practice.

Deltoids, biceps, triceps and pectorals all benefit.

Men and women do 2 sets of as many as they can manage, increasing to 3 sets.

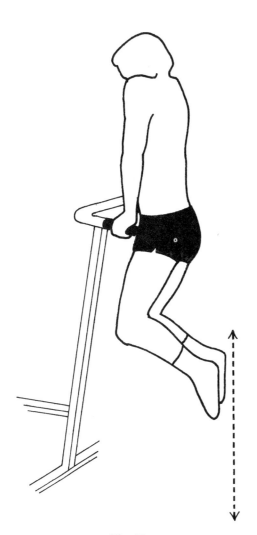

Fig 42

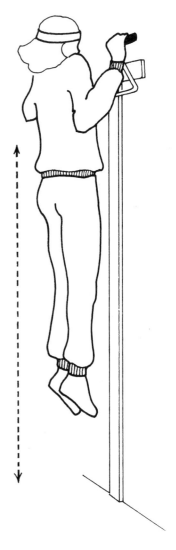

Fig 43

Exercise 44 Standing Twister

Stand on the turntable, hold rail with both hands and twist the lower body, first to the left, then to the right, keeping the upper body in line with the shoulders. Breathe freely. This exercise must be done slowly and without jerkiness.

This firms waist and upper torso and conditions the back muscles.

Men and women twist 20 times each side, increasing by 5 per week until they reach 50 each side.

Exercise 45 Seated Twister

Sit on the revolving stool and hold the rail with both hands. Twist the lower body first to the left then to the right, keeping the upper body and shoulders facing rail in line with hands. Breathe freely. This exercise must be done slowly and without jerkiness.

The effect is the same as the last exercise, and these two exercises should be done on alternate weeks.

Men and women twist 20 times each side, increasing by 5 per week until they reach 50 each side.

To cool down, do **Exercises 10 and 8.**

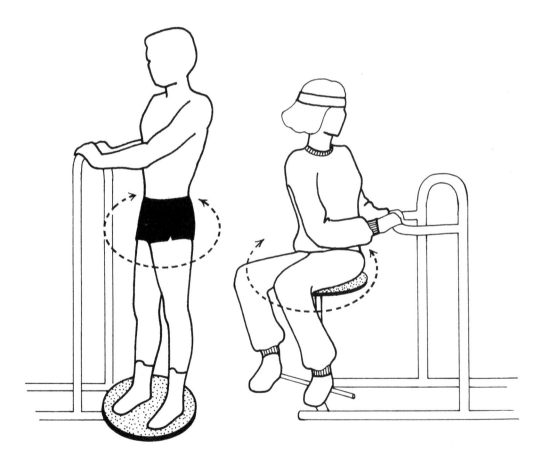

Fig 44   Fig 45

8 Extra Exercises for Specific Muscle Groups

If you are conscious of any particular weakness or area of under-development, you can, of course, build up a muscle by working to the point of resistance, as explained in Chapter 2 (How Does it Work?). Such specialisation should only be part of a full programme, however, or development might not be proportional, and in any case would not be so effective, since fitness of the whole contributes to fitness of any part.

The exercises in this chapter should therefore be added to one of the programmes in Chapter 6 or 7, and be done just before the cooling-down exercises at the end. Do the full programme, then choose not more than two or three from those you need in this chapter to get the development you want. Exercises chosen from this chapter must be done to the point of resistance.

The exercises are grouped under four headings: those for arms and shoulders; for legs; for trunk; and for abdominals. Do not attempt to do them all, but select no more than three at any one time. Do not fall into the trap of choosing those you like best, because they will probably be the ones you find easiest, and hence those you need least. The ones you find hard will develop you.

In all the exercises, men and women do 2 sets to the point of resistance, increasing to 3 sets after three months and to 4 sets after six months. Consult Chapter 2 for the weight you should use. You will see that women use lighter weights but do more repetitions. As an example of what to expect, a man's performance in three sets might be 10, 8, and 7. A woman's might be 12, 10 and 8. When a man's number in the first set rises above 12 or a woman's above 15, it is time to add a little weight to bring them back to the lower starting figure. If you do not, the work-out will take too long and will become too exhausting.

Extra Exercises for Arms and Shoulders

Exercise 46 Press Behind Neck with Barbell

Stand with the feet normal distance apart, and underneath the bar. Bend the knees, and pick up the bar, fingers over, thumbs under. Straighten knees as you lift, and take the bar over your head, to rest on the back of your neck. As the bar passes your waist level, twist your wrists, so that the bar rests on the balls of your thumbs mostly. You will need a grip slightly wider than the shoulders, in order to take the bar over your head. Palms will then be facing the front, fingers curling over the top of the bar. From this position behind the neck, press the bar upwards to arm's length, breathing out as you do so, and return to the position with the bar resting on the back of the neck, breathing in. Do the exercise with the bar only, to begin with, and progress to adding weights. The triceps benefit.

Exercise 47 Crucifix with Dumb-bells

Lie on your back on a bench with head and trunk supported, feet on floor off one end. Take a dumb-bell in each hand, and hold the arms out sideways at shoulder level with elbows slightly bent. Take a deep breath, and as you breathe out, raise the dumb-bells to arm's length above the chest. Keep the arms straight. Breathe in as you lower to the sides again. Do not let the weight drop back below the shoulders but bend elbows slightly as you lower.

Triceps and pectorals benefit.

Fig 46

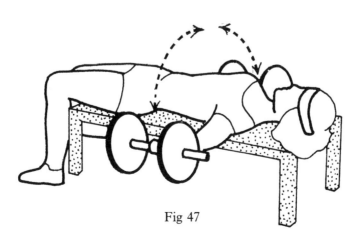

Fig 47

Exercise 48 Bent Arm Pullovers with Dumb-bell

Load the dumb-bell rod centrally. Lie on a bench as for Exercise 47, with head near the end. Grip the dumb-bell rod with as narrow a grip as possible, elbows bent, upper arms vertical, forearms at right angles, and palms facing your head. Lower the dumb-bell towards your face by bending your elbows. Breathe in as you do so, then out as you bring the weight back to the starting position over the chest.

This exercise is called a 'short range movement' and is for the triceps.

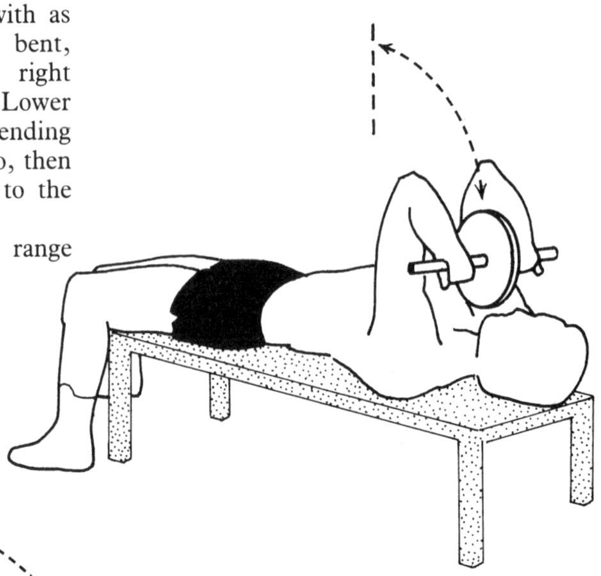

Fig 48

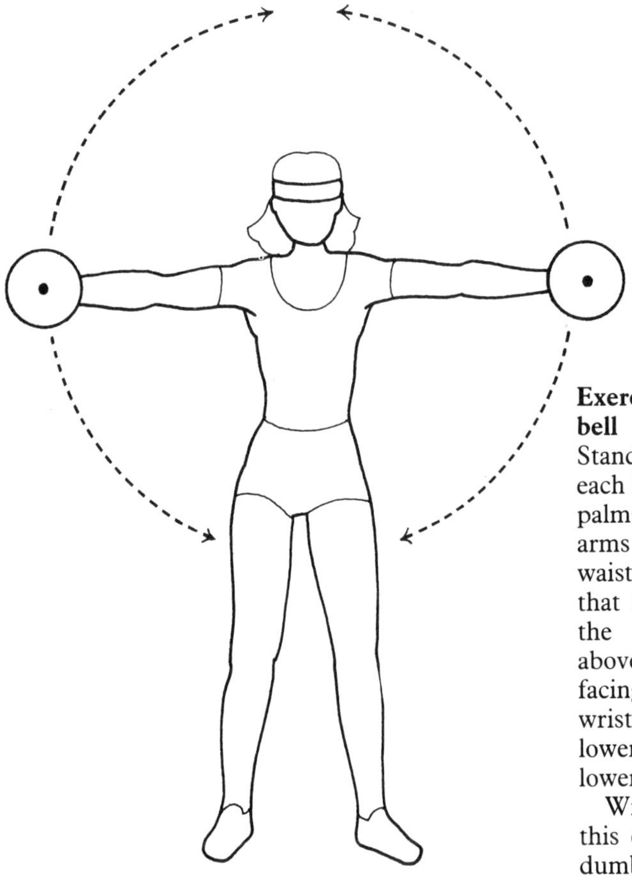

Exercise 49 Lateral Raises with Dumb-bell

Stand with feet astride. Take a dumb-bell in each hand, letting them hang down at sides, palms in towards your body. Raise your arms sideways until they are level with your waist, and at this point turn your wrists so that the palms are upwards, and carry on the movement, raising the dumb-bells above the head, when the palms will be facing each other. Make the turn of the wrists at waist level, both in raising and in lowering. Breathe out as you raise, in as you lower.

Wrists and deltoids benefit. If you find this exercise too difficult at first, take the dumb-bells up to shoulder level only, and progress until you can take them all the way up.

Fig 49

Exercise 50 Forwards and Upwards Swing with Dumb-bell

Stand upright, feet normal distance apart. Take a dumb-bell in each hand, palms facing the body, knuckles away from you, and let the hands hang in front of you touching the thighs. Raise each dumb-bell alternately, forwards and upwards to shoulder level and above your head, in one continuous movement. As you lower one hand, raise the other. Breathe freely.

Deltoids and pectorals benefit.

Exercise 51 Triceps Stretch Seated With Dumb-bell

Load the dumb-bell normally, so that you can grip it in the centre. Take it in your right hand. Sit on a bench. Raise the dumb-bell to arm's length overhead, knuckles to the front, palm to the rear. Support your upper arm with your left hand. Lower the dumb-bell behind you by bending your right elbow, maintaining the upper arm vertical. Raise the dumb-bell to arm's length again. Breathe in as you lower and out as you raise. Having done a set with the right hand, change over and do a set with the left. Use a very light dumb-bell, or the bar only to begin with, if you wish.

The triceps benefit.

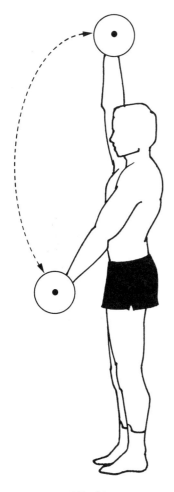

Fig 50

Fig 51

Exercise 52 Wrist Roller Exercise

For this use the wrist roller. Hold the rod, palms downwards, out in front of you, at shoulder level or just below. The weight hangs down on the end of a cord. Turn the rod towards you, so that the cord is wound round it and the weight is raised. Breathe freely.

Wrists, fingers and forearms all benefit. An alternative, if you do not have a wrist roller, is to take a sheet of newspaper in one hand, and hold it out in front of you at arm's length by one corner. Then, with the fingers, gather it up into a ball in your hand. Repeat with the other hand.

If you are doing the extra exercises for arms and shoulders at a leisure centre, the appropriate ones are:

Exercise 34 High Pulley
Exercise 39 Chest Press
Exercise 42 Dipping
Exercise 43 Chinning

Extra Exercises for the Legs

Exercise 53 Heel Raises with Barbell

Take the barbell onto the shoulders at the back of the neck as in Exercise 46. Feet are a normal distance apart. With the bar in this position, raise the heels, hold for a few seconds, then lower. Breathe out as you raise, in as you lower. It is essential in this exercise to stay upright. If it is too difficult to begin with simply do heels raise without the bar, and hold on to the back of a chair for support. Lower leg muscles and ankles benefit.

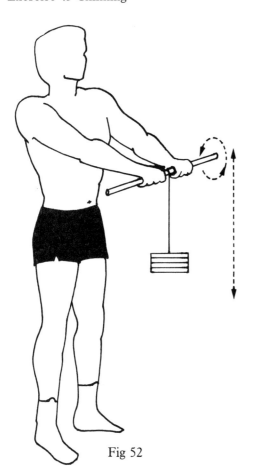

Fig 52

Fig 53

Exercise 54 Step-ups onto Bench with Weight on Shoulders
Take the barbell on your shoulders as in the last exercise. Holding it there and in good balance, step up onto a low bench or block of wood. Breathe out as you step up, in as you step back down. Try with each leg in turn being first.

Leg muscles and knee joints benefit.

Exercise 55 Leg Raise Backwards
Stand facing a wall. Place both hands against wall with body upright. Raise the left leg backward slowly by bending the knee, breathing out as you raise. Lower, breathing in. Do a set with the left leg, then repeat with the right.

Biceps of the leg benefit.

Fig 54

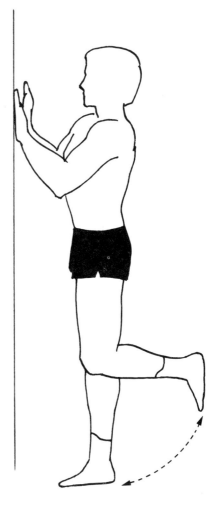

Fig 55

Exercise 56 Thigh Extension
Sit on a bench or table high enough for both legs to hang without touching the floor. Alternately straighten each leg in front of you, then lower to the hanging position again. Breathe out as you raise, in as you lower.

Leg muscles and knee joints benefit.

If you are doing your extra exercises for the legs at a leisure centre, the appropriate ones are:

Exercise 33 Thigh and Knee Leg Extension
Exercise 36 Low Pulley Thigh Pulls
Exercise 41 Leg Squat

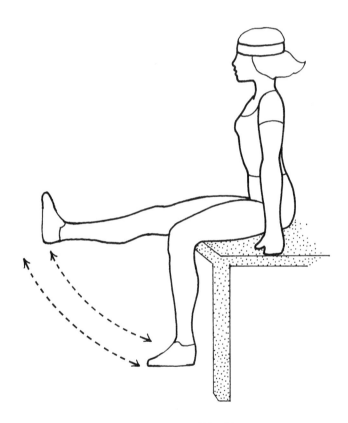

Fig 56

Extra Exercises for the Trunk

Exercise 57 Side Bends with Bar on Shoulders

Hold the bar across your shoulders at the back of your neck, with arms straight. With the bar in this position, bend as far as you can to your right, and then straighten up and bend as far as you can to your left. Breathe freely. Face the direct front during the exercise. This is a very strong trunk exercise.

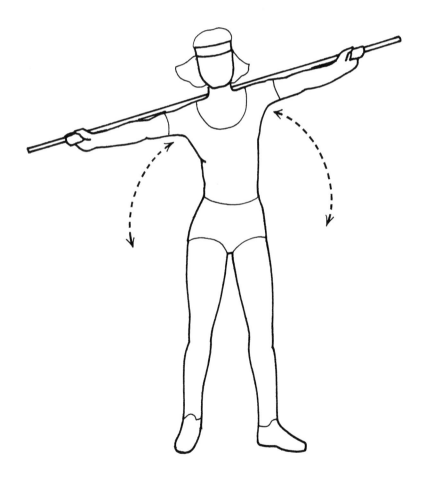

Fig 57

Exercise 58 Leg Raise Sideways

Stand by a wall. Rest the right hand on the wall, put your left hand on your hip, and slowly raise your left leg sideways as far as you can breathing out; then lower slowly, breathing in as you do so. Having done a set with the left leg, turn round and do a set with the right.

Tensor muscles and vastus externus benefit.

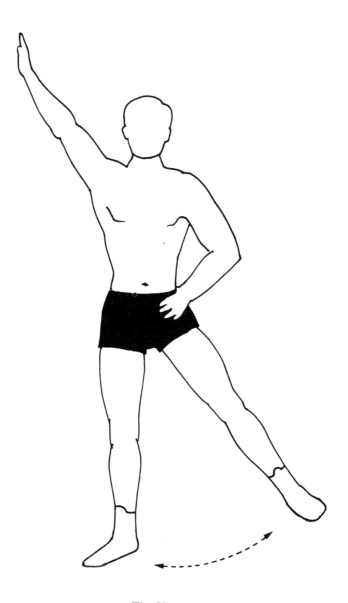

Fig 58

Exercise 59 Leg Swing

Stand sideways to the wall as in the last exercise. Rest your left hand on the wall, and your right on your hip. Swing your right foot forwards and backwards, keeping the leg straight and swinging from the hip joint. Breathe freely. Having done a set with the right leg, turn round and repeat with the left.

Hips and buttocks benefit.

If you are doing the extra exercises for the trunk at a leisure centre, the following are appropriate:

Exercise 31 Leg Press
Exercise 32 Hip Flexor
Exercise 34 High Pulley
Exercise 35 Rowing
Exercise 37 Dead Lift
Exercise 39 Chest Press
Exercise 40 Chest Bench
Exercise 42 Dipping
Exercise 43 Chinning
Exercise 44 Standing Twister
Exercise 45 Seated Twister

Extra Exercises for the Abdominals

Exercise 60 Knee Raises from Prone Position

Lie on your back. Your hands, palms down, on the floor at your sides give you some support. Raise both knees together as high as you can towards your chest, bending the knees. Breathe out as you raise them, and in as you lower them to the ground.

Abdominal muscles all benefit.

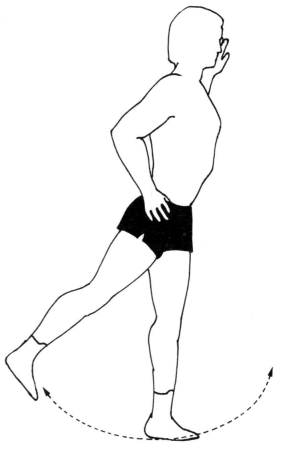

Fig 59

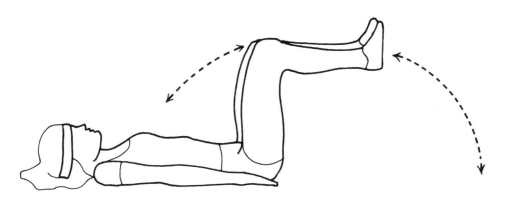

Fig 60

61

Exercise 61 Sit-Ups on Incline Bench

The incline bench can be set to various angles. Make it 30° to the horizontal to begin with. At the top of the bench is a strap. Tuck your feet in this to hold them. Lie head downwards and clasp hands at the back of your head. Now sit up, breathing out as you come up, and in as you lower back down. To make the exercise harder, you can increase the angle of the bench, but there is a limit to the angle at which you could set the bench without slipping off.

This is one of the strongest of abdominal exercises, but if you have not got an incline bench, simply do more of Exercise 17.

If you are doing extra exercises for the abdominals at a leisure centre, the appropriate ones are:

Exercise 32 Hip Flexor
Exercise 35 Rowing
Exercise 38 Abdominal Conditioner Sit-ups
Exercise 44 Standing Twister
Exercise 45 Seated Twister

You will have realised by now, in your training programmes, that the exercises benefit more muscles than the ones specifically mentioned. Your whole body becomes involved in any movement, since some muscles are holding the body at rest and others are performing the movement. The above groupings must, therefore, be taken only as general indications to the principal muscles involved.

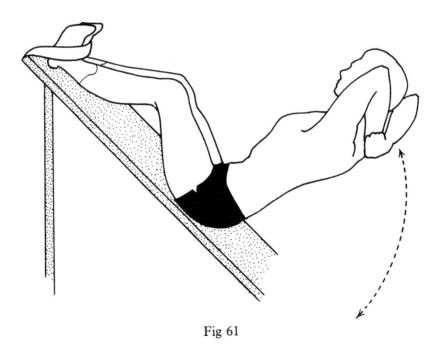

Fig 61

9 Sports and Activities Suitable for Older People

This chapter examines various sports that older people might take up, considers their benefits, and suggests the weight training exercises to improve performance in those sports. Other beneficial activities are considered that provide sufficient exercise in themselves.

Do not aim to do too much. If you are taking up a sport, reduce the number of your weight training periods to two per week and intersperse them with your sports training. Add the exercises suggested in this chapter to a programme in Chapter 6 or 7. Do not add all the suggested exercises at the same time. Try two or three per session and vary them until you find those most beneficial to you personally.

Do not work to the point of resistance. If a man, do 2 × 10 increasing to 3 × 10; if a woman 2 × 12 increasing to 3 × 12. Use light weights, as these will keep you supple. Heavy weights build strength, but they slow you down and make you less supple. Can you touch your fingers behind your back, by taking one arm over its own shoulder and the other up the back? Many weight-lifters have built up their shoulder muscles to such an extent that they can no longer do this. For most sports it would be better to retain suppleness rather than build muscle.

Suitable Sports

1 Archery
This uses shoulders and arms.
Suitable exercises are Nos **14, 15, 16 and 48** at home; **34, 37, 39, 42, 43** at a leisure centre.

2 Badminton
This uses wrists and arms and develops stamina.
Suitable exercises are Nos **11, 12, 16, 50, 52 and 54** at home; **34, 36, 41, 43, 45** at a leisure centre.

3 Bowls
Arms, shoulders and legs come into play.
Suitable exercises are Nos **15, 25, 52** at home; **31, 34, 35, 38, 52** at a leisure centre.

4 Cricket
This uses shoulders, arms, legs and abdominals.
Suitable exercises are Nos **16, 46, 49, 52, 61** at home; **31, 34, 35, 37, 38, 39, 41** at a leisure centre.

5 Fishing
Arms and Trunk need developing.
Suitable exercises are Nos **14, 16, 17, 22, 24** at home; **34, 37, 38, 39, 42** at a leisure centre.

6 Golf
This needs shoulder and arm development and suppleness of hip.
Suitable exercises are Nos **29, 30, 46, 49, 57** at home; **32, 34, 37, 43, 44** at a leisure centre.

7 Hockey
Legs and hip muscles are used.
Suitable exercises are Nos **11, 55, 56, 57, 58** at home; **32, 33, 36, 38, 41** at a leisure centre.

8 Netball

Arms, legs and stamina come into play.

Suitable exercises are Nos **14, 16, 48, 59** at home; **34, 36, 39, 41** at a leisure centre.

9 Skittles

Arms and wrists are mainly used.

Suitable exercises are Nos **15, 16, 48, 50, 52** at home; **34, 35, 39, 41, 43** at a leisure centre.

10 Squash

This is a fast game with all round benefit. Use very light weights, so that you do not impair your speed.

Suitable exercises are Nos **12, 16, 49, 51, 52, 59** at home; **32, 34, 35, 36, 43** at a leisure centre.

11 Swimming

Arms, legs and lungs benefit.

Suitable exercises are Nos **22, 23, 25, 26, 30** at home; **35, 37, 39, 40, 43** at a leisure centre.

12 Tennis and table tennis

Wrists, shoulders and general agility are developed.

Suitable exercises are Nos **16, 21, 29, 52** at home; **34, 40, 41, 43, 44** at a leisure centre.

Other Activities

Whilst not coming into the category of sports, these activities are specially suited to older people, but they do provide sufficient exercise in themselves, without the necessity of using weight training to develop for them.

1 Gardening

Anyone who has tried this knows that all muscles benefit, and there are the additional advantages of being in the open air, and growing produce.

2 Japanese martial arts

Judo, karate, aikido and ju-jitsu provide all round exercise with the additional bonus of learning something of interest and practical value. Care should be taken in the choice of club or instructor, however, as some Western clubs are very contest-orientated and some karate clubs teach full contact-karate. Older students would be better in traditional clubs, where skill rather than power is used and where karate is taught without contact.

Of similar benefit to the above is Tai Ch'i, which is a beneficial system of exercises based on martial art movements.

3 Ski-ing

This is a holiday activity, but practice can be had on dry ski slopes in some leisure centres.

4 Snooker

This is a very gentle indoor sport, but it does provide some exercise.

5 Walking

This is perhaps the safest and best activity for older people as they can go at their own pace. Three miles a day are sufficient to keep fit.

10 Specific Exercises for Slowing Down the Aging Process

In the main, the exercises in this chapter are for those in the older age groups. Some use light weights, but many are done with no apparatus.

As people grow older, their movements slow down, limbs become less supple, range of movement diminishes, and joints stiffen. There is also muscle wastage and some loss of calcium from the bones. People who continue with exercise are less susceptible to these natural manifestations of aging than others. Thus, there are quite aged Judo masters with unlined faces and with the clear smooth skin of young men.

It is best to begin to exercise as young as possible, and to keep it up, albeit in slightly diminishing measure. For those already in their later years, however, there are still some exercises that will help.

Exercises to Avoid Wrinkles in the Face

1 Push the chin forwards, then relax. 5 times.
2 Purse the lips, push them forwards, then draw them back. 5 times.
3 Shut the eyes tightly, then open them wide. 5 times.
4 Draw the eyebrows together, then part them. 5 times.
5 Smile often.

Consciously doing these simple movements twice a day will keep the skin of the face supple and the underlying muscles active and nourished. It will not get rid of existing wrinkles, but it will help to avoid their onset.

Exercises for the Neck

Sit in an upright chair to perform these.
1 Turn your head to left and then to right.
2 Look down at the floor, then up at the ceiling.
5 times each, twice a day, very gently, and never with a jerky movement, as the neck muscles are very delicate.

Exercises for the Eyes

1 Consciously look up, then down, to the left, then to the right, closing the eyes between each movement. 3 times each movement.
2 Cover the eyes with the palms for a few seconds, and think absolute blackness.
3 Give the eyes unusual work. If you mostly do close work, gaze fixedly at distant objects a few times each day.

Exercises for the Shoulders

1 Take a very light dumb-bell in each hand, and stand upright with hands hanging at sides. Now turn the palms to face front, then to face rear. 10 times each way.

2 Exercise 62

Take a bar with no weights on it, and raise it above the head as shown. Arms are close to the ears, palms to the front. From this position, pull outwards on the bar with both hands as if you were trying to stretch the bar. This is impossible, of course, but it is the effort that counts. It is called an isometric exercise. Now, push in with both hands, as if you were trying to compress the bar. Again, it is impossible, and the effort is what counts. Do 10 of each movement, then lower the bar.

If you have not got a bar, a walking stick will do just as well.

3 Exercise 63

With a bar in the hands, take the upper arms out in line with the shoulders, letting the forearms hang down with palms towards you. Now, without lowering the elbows, take the bar above your head, elbows still bent. Palms will then be facing front. Bring back to the hanging position.

The exercise will improve or maintain suppleness of the shoulder joint. If you do not have a bar, use a walking stick. Do 10 repetitions.

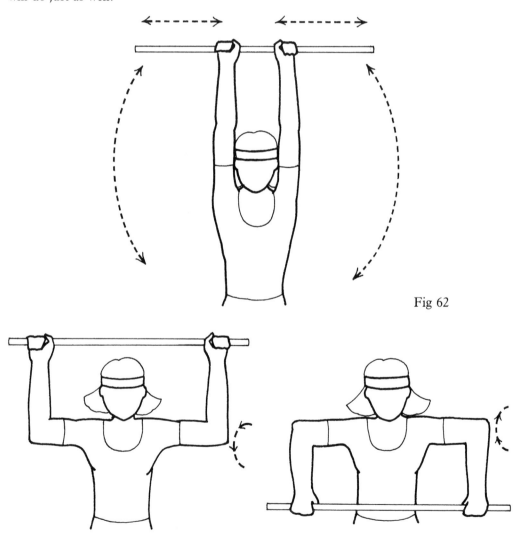

Fig 62

Fig 63 (a) and (b)

4 Exercise 64

Place your hands and forearms in contact with a wall, standing about eighteen inches away and leaning forwards to do so. From this position, push yourself upright, by straightening the elbows and pushing with the hands. The exercise is known as 'vertical press ups', and is a gentler version of the press ups described in Exercise 9. Breathe out as you press, in as you lower back to the wall. Do 10 repetitions.

Exercises for the Upper Arms

Do either:
Exercise 12 Single Hand Dumb-bell Curls, using a very light dumb-bell, or
Exercise 22 Curls with Barbell, using bar only. Men and women do 10 repetitions.

These two exercises are for the biceps. Also do either
Exercise 23 Reverse Curls with Barbell, using bar only or a walking stick, or
Exercise 13 Triceps Stretch Standing, using a very light dumb-bell or even a heavy book. Men and women do 10 repetitions.

These two exercises are for the triceps.

It is essential to balance a biceps exercise with one for the triceps, since these muscles counter-balance one another, enabling controlled movements to be made. As they grow older men find muscle wastage in the upper arms, and women tend to put on fat there. Regular and systematic use of the above exercises will help counteract this tendency.

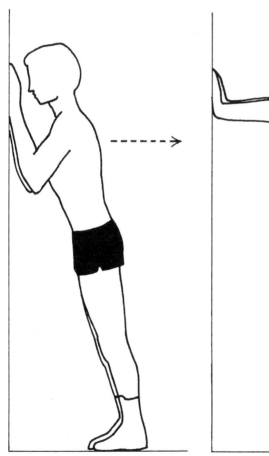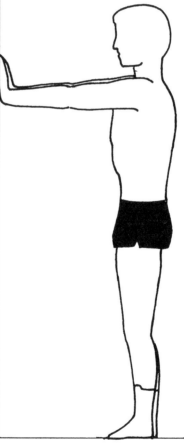

Fig 64 (a) and (b)

Exercise for the Elbows
Exercise 65

Take a bar only with no weights, or a walking stick, and hold it out in front of you, palms upwards and under the bar at shoulder height. The arms are at right angles to the upright body, and must not drop below that angle throughout the exercise. Now, bend the elbows to bring the bar towards your face, breathing out, then straighten again, breathing in. Be careful not to lower the bar below shoulder height. The movement gives suppleness to the elbow joint, and the effort of maintaining the bar at shoulder level will strengthen the elbow joint. Do 10 repetitions.

Exercises for the Forearms

1 Hold a very light dumb-bell out at arm's length in front of you. Now, turn it from palm downwards to palm upwards. 10 repetitions with each hand.

2 Hold a dumb-bell rod or a short stick out at arm's length in front of you. Now, make a wringing motion as if you were trying to wring out a dish cloth. You will not be able to twist the rod, of course; it is the effort that counts. If you are a housewife, you will probably find that you normally twist one hand towards yourself and the other away when wringing out a cloth. When doing this exercise, practise turning each hand in both directions. Do 10 times each way.

3 Exercise 66

Bend your fingers at the first and second joints, so that you can hook the fingers of one hand in the fingers of the other, when held in front of you, as shown. Now, twist the upper hand towards yourself and the lower hand away. Reverse hands and repeat. Do 10 repetitions.

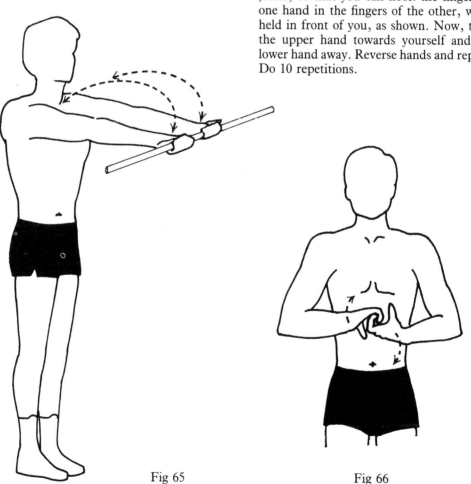

Fig 65   Fig 66

Exercises for the Wrist
1 The wrist roller (**Exercise 52**).
2 The **alternative** to the wrist roller, described under **Exercise 52.**

Exercises for the Fingers and Hands
The tendency as people grow older is for the hands to close like a claw, particularly if they are rheumatic. The main aim of these two exercises, both of which are used in karate training, is to open the hand.

1 **Exercise 67**
Hold both hands out in front of you at shoulder level. Bend the wrists back and place the top of each finger and of the thumb against its opposite number on the other hand. The points of contact are the undersides of the fingers, that is opposite the nails. Now press firmly together for a count of three, relax, then press again. Do 10 repetitions.
2 Hold both hands out in front of you at shoulder height with arms straight. Clench your fists as tightly as you can, then open your hands as widely as you can, spreading the fingers and turning the wrists back. Do 10 repetitions.

Exercises for the Hips
1 **Exercise 58** 10 repetitions each leg.
2 **Exercise 26** 10 repetitions each leg.
3 **Exercise 59** 10 repetitions each leg.
4 **Exercise 3** 10 repetitions each side.
5 **Exercise 4** 10 repetitions each side.

Exercises for the Knees
1 Lie down with the legs straight. Bend the toes of each foot upwards. The effect of this is to straighten the knee still further. 10 repetitions each leg.
2 Sit on a table with the legs hanging. Turn the toes inwards, then outwards. 10 repetitions of each.
3 **Exercise 56** 10 repetitions each leg.

Exercises for the Feet and Ankles
1 Lie flat on the ground or on a bed. Raise the heels, and with them in that position, turn the toes first inwards then outwards. 10 repetitions each way.
2 In the same position, bend the toes upwards, then point them. 10 repetitions each way.

Apart from these exercises, always wear comfortable low-heeled shoes, and expose the feet to the air each day. It helps to walk barefoot, but avoid sharp objects or stony ground.

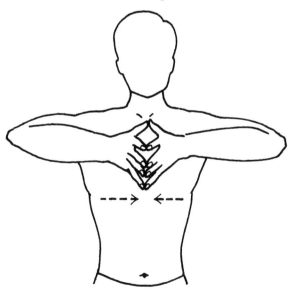

Fig 67

Exercises for the Spine

1 **Exercise 7** Do very gently and do not force yourself. 10 repetitions.

2 Stand erect and take your shoulders back. 10 repetitions.

When walking, remember the command given to soldiers, 'Head Up, Shoulders Back'. This is the same thing.

3 Sit on the floor, legs stretched in front of you. Place both hands behind your head, and as you breathe out, try to curl up into a ball. Breathe in again as you straighten back up. Do not force yourself. Do 10 repetitions.

4 **Exercise 68**

Cross the arms in front of you, place your hands on your sides, and whilst hugging your body in this position, turn as far as you can, first to left and then to right. Try to face the walls of the room on either side of you, without moving your feet. Do 10 turns each way.

One of the dangers of any form of exercise is that when it is given up, the amount of energy the body burns up in the day is reduced and at the same time the metabolic rate is lowered. This means that unless the diet is adjusted as indicated in the next two chapters, the body will put on fat.

It is improbable that a person taking up weight training in the late thirties will go on into the sixties. It is more likely that it will be given up after five to ten years, perhaps less. When giving up weight training, some other form of exercise must be substituted.

Three things are recommended:

1 Take up one of the sports or activities in Chapter 9.

2 Continue the Introductory Free-standing Programme of Chapter 5.

3 When you cannot do either of these things, select those exercises from this chapter that you think will benefit you personally.

At any age, do not over-burden yourself. Exercise should be a pleasure that leaves you feeling good, not a chore that exhausts you.

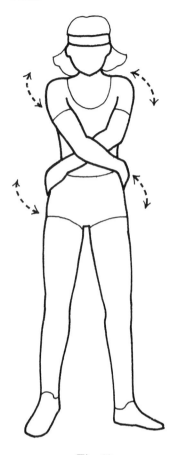

Fig 68

11 Diet and the Older Person

Up to the age of thirty-five, a person can usually get away with a somewhat haphazard lifestyle of exercise and eating, but from then onwards, the body will show signs of wear and tear, aging, and the possible onset of health problems. This is the time to re-think your lifestyle, because doing so can dictate your health for the rest of your years and determine how many of them you have left. Adopt a simple, nutritional diet. Combine it with regular exercise, and the two together will keep your muscles firm and your body young-looking, so that all your activities will remain youthful and creative.

What signs of aging do we dread? Men worry about balding and women about wrinkles. By living a healthy life style, you will look and feel as fit as possible; wrinkles will be just laughter lines and baldness a sign of maturity.

Bodies become less efficient at absorbing the goodness from food with increasing age, and therefore it is essential to include all the many and varied nutrients needed in the daily diet. It is equally important to reduce the intake of some foods which are not good and which could actually interfere with the full use of essential foods. Experts are agreed that the best chance of a fit and happy life comes from eating healthy foods, cutting out smoking, and taking regular exercise.

Improving your diet now might prevent you from developing the conditions detailed in Chapter 1.

Some general recommendations are:

1 Heart disease, high blood pressure, strokes, varicose veins and circulatory disorders benefit from taking less salt, using polyunsaturated fats, increasing dietary fibre and controlling your weight.

2 Arthritis, rheumatism, and stiffening of the joints are considered to be greatly helped by taking a simple fresh diet, low in fats and containing very little meat, also by replacing toxic drinks like tea and coffee by herbal beverages.

3 Respiratory diseases need a light nutritious diet high in Vitamin C to combat infections which would aggravate the condition. Concentrate on warm soups and stews in cold weather to prevent chills, and carefully watch your weight, as overweight people have difficulty in fully expanding their lungs and thus trap infections.

4 Certain forms of cancer are considered by some experts to be connected with a diet high in animal fats and protein. They recommend a diet high in natural wholefoods and vitamins. Again there may be more risk if you are overweight.

5 Diabetes is a metabolic failure in the pancreas to utilize carbohydrates properly. Sugar is deposited in the urine and thus lost. A diet high in unrefined carbohydrates, and hence high in fibre, may help to prevent and correct this disease, if it appears after the age of forty-five sometimes without the need for insulin.

6 Sleep can be improved by a warm milky drink before bed, and by allowing several hours to elapse after the last meal, and by avoiding such stimulants as tea, coffee and alcohol.

7 Ulcers often start between the ages of thirty and forty, usually in people of tense and nervous dispositions. Whole fresh food is recommended, and some believe that garlic and sage are useful, but life must also be taken more calmly, and plenty of time be allowed for food to be eaten leisurely.

8 Indigestion and bowel problems are often due to lack of sufficient fibre and water in the diet to stimulate the gut well enough to push the food through the entire intestinal channel. Wholemeal bread, lots of vegetables and fruit should be eaten every day. It is much better to correct the condition with diet than with laxatives.

9 Tooth decay can be halted by eating less sugar and sugary snacks.

Rejuvenation through diet is constantly being observed and reported at clinics, health resorts, and Weight Watchers classes. Students show physical changes in skin texture, elasticity of skin, lower blood cholesterol levels, improved circulation, and general well-being.

Food supplies energy, which is measured in calories. Those calories are expended in two ways:

In general metabolism, keeping warm, and in day-to-day running repairs of the body.

In activity, that is moving about.

If you consume more calories than your body can dispose of, it stores the surplus as fat.

The ways to reduce weight are:

Reduce the intake of food (energy).

Increase the rate of metabolism.

Increase activity (exercise).

Metabolism is the breaking down and using up of food by the body. Some people use everything they eat and remain the same weight; others store the extra as fat and gain weight. By increasing the metabolic rate, food is digested more efficiently. There is evidence that an increase in the heart rate leads to an increase in the metabolic rate and that it then continues to burn off energy for many hours afterwards. Therefore, the guidelines for healthier eating are:

Cut down on fats.

Eat plenty of fibre-rich food.

Use fresh rather than convenience foods.

Eat raw foods whenever possible.

Use a variety of wholegrain breads, cereals, pasta and flour.

Avoid frying in fat.

Grill, roast, poach or steam.

Cook vegetables lightly and quickly.

Avoid pastries and cakes.

Drink water; 8 to 9 pints of liquid a day are recommended.

Make these habits the basis for planning your meals. You will find planning easier if you have a knowledge of the different categories of food and of their calorific value. These categories are protein, fats, carbohydrates, dietary fibre, vitamins and minerals.

Protein People of all ages need protein. Our flesh is protein; therefore, to renew cells, heal wounds, and build muscle, we need a regular supply. Proteins are made up of small amino acids, which are found in all animal foods, such as meat, poultry, fish, eggs, cheese and yoghurt. Low-value proteins are also found in soya, wheat, nuts, potatoes, and pulse vegetables. Tofu, a soya bean curd, is a good protein food, low in fat and containing no cholesterol.

Fats Fats have an important dietary role, apart from the main one of supplying energy. They make food palatable in taste and smell; they literally 'oil' the digestive system; they are needed in the absorption of essential vitamins. All these functions can be achieved with very small amounts of fat. The main sources are: hard margarines, milk, cheese and meat for the saturated fats; soft margarines, cereals, nuts, fish and poultry for the polyunsaturated fats. Vegetable oils are recommended, such as olive, sunflower and sesame oil.

Carbohydrates All starches and sugars are carbohydrates, and these are converted into glucose and other simple sugars which are used for energy or stored as fat in the body. Most carbohydrate foods contain other nutrients, except sugar, which is purely carbohydrate. The main sources are: bread, flour, cereals, potatoes and sugar. Alcohol is used by the body as a carbohydrate.

Dietary fibre Dietary fibre comes mainly from plant cell walls, and is carbohydrate in food value. There are two types of fibre: insoluble fibre found mainly in wheat products, flour, bread, breakfast cereals, bran, and the more fibrous vegetables; and soluble fibre which is contained in all fruit and vegetables, though the richest sources are pulses, red kidney beans, baked beans, dried peas, lentils, oats and barley products. Fibre is an important part of our daily diet for several reasons: it stimulates the digestive system; it prevents constipation; it reduces the absorption of fats and sugars; it makes us feel 'full' and so reduces our appetite when we want to slim.

Vitamins Without vitamins, the body cannot make full use of the other nutrients for energy, growth and repair of body tissue. If you have a good varied diet, you will get all the vitamins you need.

Vitamin A is found in liver, cheese, milk, eggs, butter, margarine, fish liver oils, spinach, carrots and apricots. Vitamin A helps us fight infections by strengthening the cell walls to prevent bacteria and viruses from entering. It is also good for the skin and the eyesight.

Group B vitamins are found in meat, especially liver and pork, flour, bread, eggs, cheese, milk, and yeast. Folic acid, a B vitamin necessary for the formation of DNA and cell nuclei, is in offal and green vegetables. B vitamins help to break down carbohydrates, proteins and fats, and to release energy, and they are essential for the functioning of the nervous system. As B vitamins cannot be stored in the body we need a daily supply.

Vitamin C is found in green leafy vegetables, fresh fruits especially black currants, citrus fruits and potatoes. Vitamin C helps us to fight infections and to keep the skin healthy and free from dryness and wrinkles. It also helps us to absorb iron. This vitamin cannot be stored in the body, and must be included in the daily diet.

Vitamin D is found in fish liver oils, fatty fish, margarine, eggs and butter. It is also produced in the body by the action of the sun on the skin. It is needed to help us absorb and use the minerals calcium and phosphorus, which build strong bones and healthy teeth.

Vitamin E is found in most vegetable oils, cereal products, sunflower seeds and eggs. It helps in the body's use of oxygen, and is therefore invaluable to anyone doing vigorous exercise. Vitamin E is now considered to slow down the formation of certain chemicals in the cells called 'free radicals', which are the main contributors to the aging process.

Minerals A well-balanced diet should contain small amounts of different minerals, particularly calcium and iron. Calcium is vital as this forms the structure of teeth and bones, and is in constant demand. Calcium, together with magnesium, helps to reduce stress and keeps cholesterol levels down. Calcium and magnesium are found in milk, cheese, almonds, olives, kelp and other seaweed, sesame seeds, molasses, broccoli, wholegrains, yoghurt, seafoods and sea salt. Iron is needed for the formation of red blood cells which carry oxygen around the body. Oxygen is needed to produce energy, and thus is essential for the proper functioning of the body. Good sources of iron are offal, kidney, liver, shellfish, egg yolk, dark green leafy vegetables, watercress, soya, and sunflower seeds, whole grain and molasses. Zinc is another essential mineral, which might be deficient, due to modern methods of agriculture and to pollution. It is involved in the many functions of the body and a deficiency can affect the skin and permanently age it. Good natural sources are wholegrain, wheatgerm, meat, eggs, garlic, and seafood. Vegetarians especially should make sure they have enough zinc in their diet.

As you will see, certain foods crop up many times, being good sources of vitamins and minerals. Make sure that you have these regularly. They will help to protect against the effects of aging, and make a tremendous difference to your mental and physical health. Some of these recurring foods are brewers' yeast, sesame seeds, liver, wholegrains, garlic, yoghurt, sunflower seeds, and oily fish. Plan to include these in your diet. The major part of your daily intake of food should be good carbohydrate (around 65–70%), proteins (maximum 20%), and fats (maximum 15%).

Overleaf is a nutritionally balanced seven-day meal plan, based on 2,600 calories per day for men and 2,000 calories for women. You will see that it is divided into three meals per day, to allow you to absorb and digest the nutrients at regular intervals. Do not allow too long a gap between meals; the recommended time is four to five hours.

Seven-day meal plan for health

Men obtain their extra calories by adding the following items to the basic plan, each day:

2 slices of bread or 6oz (180g) potatoes.
2 fruits.
4oz/120g meat, fish or poultry.

The total of these additions is roughly 600 calories.

DAY 1

Breakfast
1 orange
1 boiled egg
1 slice wholemeal bread
2tsp margarine

Lunch
4oz/120g tuna fish
1 bread roll
1 tsp margarine
Salad of lettuce, tomato, onion, cucumber and beetroot.
2 tsp vegetable oil
1 apple

Supper
4oz/120g chicken, cooked in casserole, with 8oz/240g mixed vegetables, consisting of carrots, onions, parsnips and swedes.
6oz/180g potatoes
4oz/120g green vegetables
1 pear, topped with 1 tbsp chocolate sauce.

★   ★   ★

DAY 2

Breakfast
½ grapefruit
1oz/30g bran cereal with 2½fl oz/75ml yoghurt
1 slice wholemeal bread
2tsp margarine
2tsp marmalade

Lunch
4oz/120g cooked ham
6oz/180g mixed bean salad, with red and haricot beans, chick peas, chopped parsley, chopped onion and 2tsp oil
Lettuce
Tomato
1 slice melon

Supper
10fl oz/300ml vegetable soup, made from 1 stock cube and mixed vegetables
6oz/180g fish in breadcrumbs
4oz/120g potatoes
4oz/120g carrots
4oz/120g green vegetables
4fl oz/120ml parsley sauce
Baked apple stuffed with 1oz/30g dried fruit, topped with 2tsp honey

★   ★   ★

DAY 3

Breakfast
4oz/120ml unsweetened orange juice
3oz/90g sardines
1 slice bread
2tsp margarine
1 tomato

Lunch
10fl oz/300ml tomato juice
4oz/120g cottage cheese, topped with 1oz/30g grated hard cheese
4 crispbreads
2tsp margarine
Salad or cooked vegetables, including green vegetables, celery, onion and carrot
1 pear

Supper
3oz/90g sautéd onions
4oz/120g liver
4oz/120g spinach
2 tomatoes
4oz/120g cooked brown rice
6oz/180g fresh fruit salad
2½fl oz/75ml natural yoghurt

★   ★   ★

DAY 4

Breakfast
5oz/150g grapes
1 scrambled egg
1 tomato
1 slice wholemeal bread
2tsp margarine

Lunch
Macaroni cheese, using 4oz/120g cooked macaroni, 3oz/90g grated cheese, 4oz/120g mushrooms, 4oz/120g cauliflower, 5fl oz/150ml white sauce, topped with 2tsp sesame seeds
4oz/120g green beans
1 orange

An alternative packed lunch would be:
3oz/90g cheese
2oz/60g bread roll, with sesame seeds
2tsp margarine
Mixed salad
1 orange

Supper
6oz/180g mackerel (canned or fresh)
4oz/120g sautéd potatoes
4oz/120g peas
1 large green salad
6oz/180g stewed fruit
2½fl oz/75ml yoghurt

      ★   ★   ★

DAY 5

Breakfast
1 banana
1½oz/45g muesli
5fl oz/150ml yoghurt
1 slice wholemeal bread
2tsp margarine
1tsp marmite
1 tomato

Lunch
4oz/120g baked beans
1 egg
1oz/30g grated cheese
1oz wholemeal bread
Large mixed salad
2tsp mayonnaise
6oz/180g pineapple

Supper
6oz/180g salmon (fresh or tinned)
Cucumber
4oz/120g corn on the cob
3oz/90g green beans
Sliced green pepper
4 crispbreads
2tsp margarine
1 orange set in 5fl oz/150ml jelly

      ★   ★   ★

DAY 6

Breakfast
½ grapefruit
1 slice bacon
1 egg
1 tomato
1 slice wholemeal bread with 2tsp margarine

Lunch
6oz/180g jacket potato or bread roll, filled with 4oz/120g shrimps, garnished with chopped parsley
2tsp mayonnaise
Lettuce, cucumber, tomato, grated carrot, chopped celery
1 pear

Supper
4oz/120g turkey
1oz/30g herb stuffing
4oz/120g cooked pasta, mixed with 3oz/90g cooked peas and 3oz/90g chopped green peppers
4oz/120g spinach
5oz/150g blackcurrants
2½fl oz/75ml yoghurt

      ★   ★   ★

DAY 7

Breakfast
4oz/120g pineapple
1½oz/45g porridge (uncooked weight)
5fl oz/150ml milk
2tsp honey
1 slice wholemeal bread
2tsp margarine

Lunch
4oz/120g beef
3oz/90g Yorkshire pudding
4oz/120g baked jacket potato
4oz/120g spring greens
4oz/120g carrots
2fl oz/60ml gravy
1 slice apple pie
5fl oz/150ml custard

Supper
4oz/120g canned drained pilchards
Mixed salad of lettuce, tomato, cucumber and spring onions
2tsp mayonnaise
2 crispbreads
2 plums

A few other points:
Use 1pt/600ml skimmed milk, or ½pt/300ml full cream milk every day, and up to 5fl oz/150ml yoghurt as well, if desired. This milk allowance includes that used in both drinks and in cooking.

Try to cut down sugar to a minimum. Remember 1oz/30g will add 112 calories to your diet. If alcohol is drunk, this too will add calories. 10fl oz/300ml beer is approximately 90 calories, and a glass of wine 80 calories.

Tea or coffee may be drunk as desired.

If you wish, you may add to the above menus, 1 sweet biscuit, or 1 cake, or 1 bun, or 2oz/60g sweets or chocolates each day.

Eat at least one serving of green vegetables every day. Remember that fresh fruit and vegetables provide more vitamins than the same quantities when cooked.

If you would prefer to eat more often than the three meals suggested in the above plan, omit items as required from the meal plan and eat when you need them, but do not alter the total amounts. For example, you could have fruit at mid-morning or in the evening, or a slice of bread as a tea-time sandwich. Do not forget that raw vegetables such as carrots, cucumber, celery, hard cabbage, green and red peppers etc are very useful 'fillers'. They add a negligible number of calories, but are nutritionally excellent.

If you plan your week's meals along the lines suggested, you will soon feel fitter and look trimmer, and you will have more energy because your body will be getting all the nutrients it needs.

There are so many cookery books that it would be out of place to fill this one with recipes, but a few that are useful and not generally found elsewhere are given below.

Recipe for Main Course Soup (2 servings)
Ingredients:
3oz/90g uncooked lentils
16fl oz/480ml water
6oz/180g diced scrubbed raw potato
3oz/90g chopped onions
3oz/90g chopped carrots
3oz/90g chopped celery
1 beef stock cube
2tbsp chopped parsley
1 crushed clove of garlic
1 bay leaf
Black pepper

Method:
Boil lentils in water for 20 minutes over gentle heat. Add remaining ingredients, and continue cooking gently in covered pan, until potato is tender (approximately 30 minutes). Remove bay leaf before serving.

Recipe for Chicken Liver Pâté
Ingredients:
12oz/360g chicken livers
Juice of 1 lemon
4tsp Worcester sauce
½tsp nutmeg
½tsp salt
2 slices wholemeal breadcrumbs

Method:
Place the first five ingredients into a saucepan and cook gently for 10 minutes. Stir in breadcrumbs and combine in blender. Chill for ½ hour before serving.

Recipe for Home Made Muesli
Ingredients:
1tbsp oatmeal (soak overnight) or 1 tbsp oatflakes (soak 10 minutes)
4tbsp water
1 large apple
1tbsp chopped nuts
Either 1oz/30g dried fruit or ½ banana or 2oz/60g soft fruit
3tbsp natural yoghurt or 4fl oz/120ml milk
1tsp honey

Method:
Soak oats in water. Grate unpeeled apple onto oats and add remaining ingredients.

Recipe for Easy Salad Dressing
2tbsp cider or wine vinegar
1tbsp sunflower oil
½tsp dried mustard
½tsp honey
Place ingredients in screw top jar and shake well.

Recipe for Yoghurt Dressing
1tbsp mayonnaise
2tbsp natural yoghurt
Grated rind of 1 orange
1tsp herbs, such as sage, thyme or mint.

12 Slimming and Weight Control

One of the most common problems with approaching middle age is that weight goes on very easily, and this makes us feel and look older, less energetic and less attractive. Without realising it, fewer calories are probably used in energy output, and at the same time the diet contains slightly more and slightly richer foods. Adding one extra biscuit a day to the normal diet can put on ten pounds in a year. Driving half a mile to the station every day instead of walking can add half a stone in a year.

The obvious solution is to take more exercise and to plan food intake, so as to eat only what is required for nutritional needs and no more. This is the answer to a long and healthy life.

Many people believe that health and life-span are largely in our own hands. There is no doubt that to be the correct weight for height and build, with all joints and muscles moving easily and blood flowing freely through uncluttered veins, gives the best chance of a long and active life. So many problems are made worse by being overweight, and just by changing eating and exercise pattern it is possible to avoid them.

Chapter 11 explained what foods would best guard against the health problems of people over thirty-five, and gave guidelines to healthier eating. What else is needed in order to lose weight?

There are five points:

1 Restore the ritual to eating; regular mealtimes help the digestion to work more efficiently.

2 Study calorific values of food, and plan a balanced intake of exactly what you need.

3 Re-organise your food store. Use a large fruit and vegetable rack, a small bread bin, and hide your biscuit barrel. You will not need it.

4 Study the height and weight chart in Chapter 2 and see what weight you should be. This chapter will help you to achieve that goal weight. Do not think because you are forty or fifty that an increase in weight is inevitable. That is losing the fight before the first round.

5 Learn to say 'No'. When you have studied this chapter, you will know what you ought to be eating, and if you insist on sticking to the plan, you will soon earn the respect of those who would tempt you to have a little more of something.

As the energy value of food is measured in calories, it is important to understand what this means exactly in terms of what you are going to eat. The recognised energy equivalents of food are as follows:

1oz/30g carbohydrate provides nearly 110 calories

1oz/30g fat provides nearly 260 calories

1oz/30g protein provides just over 110 calories

1 fl oz/30ml alcohol provides nearly 200 calories.

Most foods contain a mixture of nutrients, with the other components of minerals, vitamins and water providing no calories, so the calorific value of any food is calculated by the carbohydrate, fat, protein and alcohol content.

The amount of energy in calories you will need to maintain your correct weight will depend on sex, age and weight. A man uses up slightly more energy than a woman of the same weight. Younger people use up more energy than older people. Heavier people use up more energy than lighter people.

Certain illnesses can make us use more energy, as can pregnancy and nursing babies. The more active your way of life, the more energy you will use.

A table prepared by the DHSS indicates, in broad outline, that a man between the ages of thirty-five and sixty-five with a sedentary occupation will need 2,600 calories per day. A woman in the same age group and similar occupation will need 2,000 calories per day. This is the basis of the Seven Day Meal Plan for Health in the last chapter. But to slim, you have to cut down on that.

A calorie chart is worth using, as it will deter you when you are tempted to snack on a handful of nuts, a packet of crisps, or a bar of chocolate. You can see that any one of these would add 200 calories to your intake, and the effect would be gone in a flash. You would have done much better to use those calories for more nutritional foods that would have satisfied your appetite longer. Study the chart below. It is a good guide.

Calorie Chart

Meat

	Weight	Calories
Bacon, 1 grilled back rasher	1oz/30g	80
Beef, sirloin roast	1oz/30g	50
Beefburger, large grilled	4oz/120g	240
Corned beef	1oz/30g	60
Ham, boiled lean	1oz/30g	47
Lamb, leg roast	1oz/30g	54
Liver pâté	1oz/30g	90
Pork, joint roast	1oz/30g	56
Salami	1oz/30g	130
Sausage, beef, large grilled	1oz/30g	130

Poultry, game, offal

	Weight	Calories
Chicken, roast, meat only	1oz/30g	42
Duck, roast, meat only	1oz/30g	54
Heart, roast, ox	1oz/30g	50
Kidney, lamb's fried	1oz/30g	65
Liver, lamb's fried	1oz/30g	66
Rabbit, stewed	1oz/30g	51
Turkey, roast	1oz/30g	40

Fish

	Weight	Calories
Cod, baked or grilled	1oz/30g	27
Crab, canned	1oz/30g	25
Haddock, fillet fried in breadcrumbs	1oz/30g	50
Herring, grilled on the bone	1oz/30g	38
Kipper fillet, grilled or baked	1oz/30g	58
Mackerel	1oz/30g	53

	Weight	Calories
Pilchards, canned in tomato sauce	1oz/30g	36
Prawns, boiled shelled	1oz/30g	30
Salmon, steamed or poached	1oz/30g	56
Sardines, canned in tomato sauce	1oz/30g	50
Shrimps	1oz/30g	33
Trout, grilled or poached on the bone	1oz/30g	25
Tuna, drained of oil	1oz/30g	60
Fish fingers, grilled	1oz/30g	60

Eggs

	Weight	Calories
Eggs, size 3 boiled or poached	—	80
Egg, fried	—	100
Omelette, 2 eggs	—	160

Green and salad vegetables

	Weight	Calories
Beans, runner boiled	1oz/30g	5
Beetroot	1oz/30g	12
Brussels sprouts, boiled	1oz/30g	5
Cabbage	1oz/30g	4
Carrots, raw	1oz/30g	6
Cauliflower	1oz/30g	3
Celery, raw	1oz/30g	2
Cucumber	1oz/30g	3
Lettuce, raw	1oz/30g	3
Mushrooms, raw	1oz/30g	4
Onions, raw	1oz/30g	7
Peas, boiled	1oz/30g	15
Peppers, raw	1oz/30g	4
Spinach	1oz/30g	9
Spring greens, boiled	1oz/30g	4
Tomatoes, raw	1oz/30g	4

Low-calorie drinks

	Weight	Calories
Bovril, 1tsp	—	10
Marmite, 1tsp	—	10
Coffee, no milk or sugar	—	—
Orange juice, unsweetened	5fl oz/150ml	50
Oxo cube, meat	—	15
Tea, no milk or sugar	—	—
Tomato juice	5fl oz/150ml	20
Water	—	—

Fruit

	Weight	Calories
Apple, raw	1oz/30g	10
Apricot, fresh with stone	1oz/30g	7
Banana, flesh only	1oz/30g	22
Blackberries, raw	1oz/30g	8
Blackcurrants	1oz/30g	8
Cherries, fresh with stones	1oz/30g	12
Dates, dried without stones	1oz/30g	70
Gooseberries, ripe dessert	1oz/30g	10

Grapes, white	1oz/30g	17	Kidney beans, red boiled	1oz/30g	25
Lemon, whole		15	Carrots, raw	1oz/30g	6
Melon, with skin	1oz/30g	4	Leeks, raw weight	1oz/30g	9
Orange, large		75	Lentils, raw weight	1oz/30g	86
Peach, fresh with stone	1oz/30g	9	Lentils, boiled weight	1oz/30g	28
Pear, whole	1oz/30g	8	Onions, raw	1oz/30g	7
Pineapple, fresh, flesh only	1oz/30g	13	Parsnips, raw	1oz/30g	14
Prunes, stewed with stones,			Potatoes, baked with skins	1oz/30g	24
no sugar	1oz/30g	21	Swedes	1oz/30g	6
Raisins, sultanas, currants	1oz/30g	70	Sweetcorn, canned in brine	1oz/30g	22
Raspberries, fresh	1oz/30g	7	Sweetcorn, whole medium		
Rhubarb, uncooked weight	1oz/30g	2	cob	—	155
Strawberries, fresh	1oz/30g	7	Turnips	1oz/30g	6

Cereals

Bran-enriched cereals	1oz/30g	80
Cornflakes	1oz/30g	100
Muesli	1oz/30g	110
Porridge	1oz/30g	105

Milk

Milk, whole	1fl oz/30ml	20
Milk, skimmed	1fl oz/30ml	10
Custard	¼pt/120ml	175
Ice cream	1fl oz/30ml	50
Rice pudding	6oz/180g	160
Yoghurt, fruit	5fl oz/150ml	175
Yoghurt, low fat	1oz/30g	15
Yoghurt, whole milk	1oz/30g	25

Cheese

Brie	1oz/30g	88
Cheddar	1oz/30g	120
Cottage	1oz/30g	27
Cream	1oz/30g	125
Curd	1oz/30g	54
Edam	1oz/30g	90
Stilton	1oz/30g	131

Bread

Bread, white	1oz/30g	66
Crispbread	1 slice	30
Wheatgerm	1oz/30g	65
Wholemeal	1oz/30g	61

Rice and pasta

Pasta, macaroni, wholewheat		
boiled	1oz/30g	33
Rice, brown boiled	1oz/30g	33

Root vegetables and pulses

Baked beans in tomato sauce	1oz/30g	20
Butter beans, boiled	1oz/30g	27

Fats

Butter	1oz/30g	210
Lard	1oz/30g	253
Margarine	1oz/30g	210
Margarine, low-fat spread	1oz/30g	105
Mayonnaise	1fl oz/30ml	205
Oil, sunflower	1fl oz/30ml	255
Peanut butter	1oz/30g	177
Salad cream, low calorie	½fl oz/15ml	45

Biscuits, cakes, pastry

Biscuit, plain digestive	—	70
Chocolate biscuit	—	130
Semi-sweet rich tea biscuit	—	50
Cake, plain fruit	4oz/120g	360
Cake, sponge	3oz/90g	400
Currant bun		250
Danish pastry	1	239
Date and nut bread	1 slice	215
Doughnut with jam	2oz/60g	200
Oat cakes	1	45
Pastry, flaky	1oz/30g	160
Pastry, short	1oz/30g	150
Pie, apple	6oz/180g	300
Pie, steak and kidney	8oz/240g	735
Sausage roll, flaky pastry	2oz/60g	270
Scone	1oz/30g	100
Yorkshire pudding	1oz/30g	60

Sugar, sweets, chocolates, preserves

Chocolate	1oz/30g	130
Golden syrup	1oz/30g	84
Honey	1oz/30g	82
Jam or marmalade	1oz/30g	74
Sugar	1oz/30g	112
Sweets, boiled	1oz/30g	105
Toffees	1oz/30g	130

Cream

Clotted	1fl oz/ 30ml	165
Double	1fl oz/ 30ml	127
Single	1fl oz/ 30ml	60

Crisps and nuts

Crisps, potato	1oz/30g	150
Peanuts, roasted	1oz/30g	162
Sesame seeds	1tbsp	55
Tofu (soya bean curd)	1oz/30g	16

Alcoholic drinks

Beer	½pt	85
Cider	½pt	100
Spirits – brandy, gin, rum, vodka, whisky	25ml	50
Wine, dry	4fl oz	75
Wine, sweet	4fl oz	105

How can we economise on calories? Consider the various foods.

Meat Always remove all fat and skin. Remember that turkey and chicken are lower in fat than beef, lamb, pork, goose, and duck. Liver, kidney and heart contain very little fat. Sausages, beefburgers and faggots contain higher proportions of fat than lean meat. Salami, garlic sausages, pâtés and luncheon meats are all higher in fats than cold meats. When using minced meat, start by gently frying until the fat becomes liquid and can be poured off.

Fish Eat white fish, such as cod, plaice, hake and haddock; oily fish such as mackerel and herring are higher in calories. Do not use batter-coated frozen fish, which needs frying. When possible, select the canned fish in brine not oil. If your sardines, pilchards, tuna or mackerel are canned in oil, drain off before using and before assessing the weight. Shellfish is low in calories.

Eggs With egg dishes, most of the fat is in the yolk, so remember that the yolk contains the calories not the white.

Milk Must be included in your diet, as it is a complete food, but use skimmed or powdered milk. Cream is very high in fat and to be avoided when slimming. Natural yoghurt is a good alternative to cream; a small carton contains 75 calories, but sweetened fruit yoghurts can contain up to 175 calories.

Fats All fats are very high in calories, so only a small amount is needed each day. Low-fat spreads contain half the calories of margarine. Grilling food instead of frying will remove extra fat. See, too, the recipe for low calorie salad dressing in the last chapter.

Cheeses Hard cheeses are high in fat and therefore in calories, and must be eaten sparingly. Choose low-fat cheeses such as cottage and curd cheese, as these are a valuable source of protein.

Vegetables Contain a high percentage of water, but also supply a considerable quantity of essential nutrients, so are extremely important to your slimming plan. Green leaf vegetables have virtually no calories, root vegetables very few. Because vegetables are bulky and slow down our eating, they make us feel full. Frying vegetables will multiply their calorie count three or four times, so boil, bake, steam or purée them, and eat the skin or rind whenever possible. Beans, peas, and sweetcorn have a particularly high fibre content. See the recipe for a main soup course in the previous chapter.

Fruit The sweeter the fruit the more calories it contains. If sugar is used to sweeten stewed fruit, the calories are greatly increased, so use a low-calorie sweetener instead.

Bread Eat a variety of breads. Wholemeal and bran-enriched breads provide extra fibre in the diet. Low-calorie breads contain more air, so they have fewer calories per slice.

Breakfast cereals The unsweetened lightweight cereals and porridge are lowest in calories. If you must sweeten them, use a sugar substitute or a little honey, and always count the milk or yoghurt added to your cereal as part of your daily allowance. See the recipe for home made muesli in the previous chapter.

Rice and pasta Useful additions to your diet, but fried rice greatly increases the calorific value. Brown rice and wholemeal pasta are good sources of fibre.

Biscuits and cakes Best forgotten when slimming. If you cannot do without them eat small plain wholemeal biscuits.

Sugar Is not needed nutritionally, and it is better to cut it out altogether. By doing this, you will lose your 'sweet tooth', and will enjoy the flavour of foods without adding sugar. If you really must have sweetening, use a sugar substitute.

Alcohol Alcoholic drinks are best cut out when slimming. They provide no nutrient value. Choose low-calorie soft drinks or mineral water; instead.

These hints will help you to reduce your calories, but to seriously set about slimming, you need a plan.

On the next page is given a Seven-day Slimmers' Meal Plan. It has an inbuilt discipline, and will give you the confidence of knowing that your lower calorie meals are still providing all the nutrients your body needs. It should also leave you feeling satisfied.

If you want to nibble between meals, eat raw vegetables. They will exercise the jaws, fill the gap, and add very few calories.

If you have to take meals to work, use a plastic container, screw top jar, or vacuum flask. Weigh all portions carefully, and note that spoon measurements mean level, not heaped up spoon. Where 2tsp low-fat spread is listed, you can change this to 1tsp of polyunsaturated margarine. You may substitute skimmed milk for natural yoghurt (5fl oz/150ml yoghurt equals ½pt/ 300ml skimmed milk). Since herbs and spices contain no calories and they improve the flavour of recipes so much, they can be used freely.

You may interchange lunch and supper menus, but try to have the total foods listed in one day on that day.

Using this meal plan with increased exercise, you will lose the extra weight and flabbiness, and when you reach your goal you will be firm and trim as well as slim. You can expect a weight loss of at least 1lb per week; 2lb is really good.

It is helpful to keep a record of what you eat. Make up your own meal plans, using the quantities and varieties in the above plan with the calorie chart as a guide. You will find it fun and be helped to stick to your calorie limit.

When you have reduced to your correct weight, add 50 calories per day to the Slimmers' Meal Plan, so that you gradually return to the Seven Day Meal Plan for Health (Chapter 11), but as soon as your weight starts to creep up again, stop adding calories, as you have found the number necessary for you to maintain your body at its current activity level.

Make sure that you include in your slimming diet the following items, every day:

1pt/600ml skimmed milk, either liquid or powdered, or ½pt/300ml skimmed milk and 5fl oz/150ml natural yoghurt.
3 fruits (if a woman) or 5 fruits (if a man)
At least one green vegetable, as well as salads and cooked vegetables.
Meat, fish, poultry, eggs, cheese or pulses in at least two meals.
Bread, cereals, pasta.
Small quantities of fat, to be eaten with meals, eg margarine, or salad cream or oil.

Seven-day Slimmers' Meal Plan for Men and Women

This is based on 1,200 calories per day for women and 1,800 for men. Men obtain the extra 600 calories by adding every day the following items:

2 slices of bread, or 6oz/180g potatoes
2 fruits
4oz/120g of meat, fish or poultry.

DAY 1

Breakfast
1 orange
1 boiled egg
1oz/30g wholemeal bread
2tsp low-fat spread

Lunch
3oz/90g tuna fish
Salad of lettuce, onion rings and tomato
2 celery sticks
1oz/30g beetroot
2tsp salad cream
2 crispbreads (50 calories)
1 apple

Supper
3oz/90g chicken without skin cooked in casserole with
    3oz/90g carrots
    4oz/120g onions
    2oz/60g parsnips
    3oz/90g turnips
3oz/90g jacket potato
4oz/120g cooked green vegetables
1 pear

⋆　　⋆　　⋆

DAY 2

Breakfast
½ grapefruit
1oz/30g bran cereal
2½fl oz/75ml natural yoghurt
1 slice wholemeal bread
2tsp low-fat spread

Lunch
3oz/90g lean ham
3oz/90g mixed bean salad, using red, haricot, chick etc

1tsp chopped parsley
2oz/60g chopped onion
Salad of lettuce, tomato, cucumber and celery
2tsp vegetable oil
1 medium slice melon

Supper
Vegetable soup using 1 stock cube and 6oz/180g celery, onion and carrot
4oz/120g white fish cooked in 4fl oz/120ml skimmed milk, thickened with 1tsp chopped parsley and 1tsp cornflower
4oz/120g green beans
1tsp margarine
1 baked apple cooked in 2tbsp low-calorie lemon drink

⋆　　⋆　　⋆

DAY 3

Breakfast
4fl oz/120ml unsweetened orange or grapefruit juice
2oz/60g drained sardines
1oz/30g bread
2tsp low-fat spread
1 tomato

Lunch
4oz/120g cottage cheese
2 crispbreads (50 calories)
Salad of 1 tomato, celery, cucumber, carrot, shredded cabbage, onion, pepper.
2tsp low-fat spread
1 banana, medium sized

Supper
3oz/90g sautéd onion in 2tsp vegetable oil. Add 3oz/90g liver and cook for 7 minutes
3oz/90g cooked brown rice
4oz/120g spinach
1 tomato
4oz/120g mushrooms
4oz/120g fresh fruit salad
2½fl oz/75ml natural yoghurt

⋆　　⋆　　⋆

DAY 4

Breakfast
4oz/120g grapes
1 scrambled egg
1 tomato
1oz/30g bread
2tsp low-fat spread

Lunch

Macaroni cheese, using 3oz/90g cooked macaroni, 3oz/90g mushrooms, 3oz/90g cauliflower, 2oz/60g grated cheese, combined with 2fl oz/60ml skimmed milk. Sprinkle the top with 1tsp sesame seeds.

Serve with a mixed salad of lettuce, tomato, celery and chives.

1 orange

An alternative packed lunch would be:
2oz/60g cheese
2oz/60g bread roll
Mixed salad
2tsp low-fat spread
1 orange

Supper

3oz/120g tuna fish
2oz/60g sautéd potatoes
Large green salad
4oz/120g stewed fruit
2½fl oz/75ml natural yoghurt

★　　★　　★

DAY 5

Breakfast

3oz/90g stewed prunes with their juice
1½oz/45g muesli
5fl oz/150ml natural yoghurt

Lunch

3oz/90g baked beans
1 egg
1oz/30g bread
2tsp low-fat spread
Mixed salad of grated cabbage, onion, carrots, celery and pepper
4oz/120g pineapple

Supper

4oz/120g salmon, fresh or tinned
Cucumber
2oz/60g corn on the cob
2oz/60g green beans
2oz/60g peppers
2tsp low-fat spread
1 orange

★　　★　　★

DAY 6

Breakfast

½ grapefruit
1 poached egg on 1 slice bread
1 tomato
3oz/90g mushrooms
2tsp low-fat spread

Lunch

3oz/90g cooked jacket potato, or 2oz/60g bread roll, filled with 3oz/90g shrimps
Chopped parsley
2tsp salad cream
Large mixed salad of lettuce, celery, cucumber, tomato, spring onions, and pepper
1 pear

Supper

4oz/120g turkey, no skin
3oz/90g cooked pasta mixed with 2oz/60g cooked peas and 2oz/60g cooked celery and 1tbsp chopped chives or spring onions and 1tsp vegetable oil
4oz/120g spinach
5oz/150g blackcurrants
2½fl oz/75ml natural yoghurt

★　　★　　★

DAY 7

Breakfast

4oz/120g pineapple
1oz/30g porridge (uncooked weight)
5fl oz/150ml skimmed milk
2tsp honey

Lunch

3oz/90g lean beef
3oz/90g jacket potato
2tsp low-fat spread
4oz/120g spring greens
3oz/90g carrots
3oz/90g boiled parsnips
5oz/150g strawberries
2½fl oz/75ml natural yoghurt

Supper

3oz/90g drained canned pilchards
Mixed salad of lettuce, tomato, celery, cucumber and peppers
3 crispbreads
2tsp low-fat spread
4oz/120g plums

Exercises for Slimming

It has been found that static exercises such as weight training are not as effective for slimming as the non-static ones, such as jogging, running, games, rowing or cycling. If going out and doing these does not appeal to you or is impractical in your circumstances, two very popular methods of getting the same kind of exercise in the home are the rowing machine and the exercise bike. We know several people over seventy who use exercise bikes. One, who has a heart pace-maker, told us that she had 'cycled round the world' in equivalent miles on her bike, and her weight had been kept down and her heart condition improved thereby.

If you do not wish to buy the apparatus, many gyms and leisure centres have them as part of the equipment. Try one or the other; there is no need to have both.

Exercise 69 Rowing Machine

If buying a machine, choose one that has a smooth gliding action, shock absorbers, and an adjustable pulling resistance. Some models can be used in a sitting or standing position and provide a variety of exercises.

Basically, the machine is a sliding seat running along rails, with oars that you pull against resistance. Pulling the oars exercises the arms, shoulders, chest and back; pressing against the foot rest and straightening and bending the legs exercises all the leg muscles; and the bending forwards and pulling back exercises the abdominals, so that the machine provides an all-round work-out.

Men and women start with 5 minutes, twice a day for the first week, and then build up to two periods a day for as long as they feel able. To shorten the time taken by the exercise, add to the resistance you are pulling against, and do not over-exhaust yourself. You should aim to increase your pulse rate and be pleasantly out of breath each time.

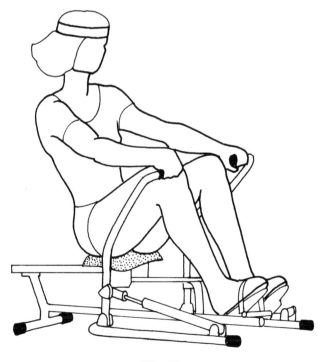

Fig 69

Exercise 70 Exercise Bike

There are many bikes to choose from, at varying prices. Try to select one that has an adjustable resistance, speedometer, timer, and an arm and shoulder exercise incorporated into the handlebars. Then, as you exercise the legs and abdominals by cycling, you can also pull the handlebars towards you and release the pressure to exercise arms, shoulders, back and chest.

To improve leg muscles, cycle against a hard resistance.

To improve stamina, circulation or the heart muscles, use light resistance and cycle for longer periods.

Sit comfortably upright on the machine. Do not lean over the handlebars as on a racing bicycle. Use your machine by an open window or outdoors if possible, and if you get bored just cycling, read a book balanced on the handlebars or listen to the radio, as you cycle.

Men and women start with 5 minutes per day for the first week, then increase to two periods of 5 minutes per day. Following that, add 5 minutes per day, spread between the two periods, until you are doing 15 or 20 minutes per day. This is considered a good programme. If you want to do more, there is no reason why you should not; if you want to do less, increase the resistances you are working against. Generally, however, slimming is best helped by low resistances and longer cycling time.

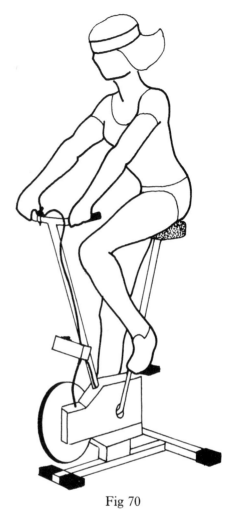

Fig 70

13 The Psychology of Training

Take a good look at yourself. Are you satisfied with what you see? Let us face it, in most career structures, forty is old today, and if you have not reached your goal by thirty-five or soon after, you should accept that you have reached your true level. If you are well established, there may be another step or two up the promotion ladder ahead; again some exceptional individuals do change direction with success; but the majority will coast along as they are until retirement comes.

Most people are happy with that. The frustrations and conflicts of the teens are over; education, training and early marital problems have been surmounted; there may still be dependent children, but soon they will leave home. Now is the time to look at your own life style and see what would add to its enjoyment.

Whatever position you have reached and whatever future you see ahead, ill health would undermine everything. In your self-examination, ask yourself whether you are overweight, whether you take enough exercise, if you work too hard, if you allow yourself enough recreation and if you enjoy life. Your future can bring happiness. You are probably better off financially at thirty-five than you were at twenty-five; you will probably be happily married and have more leisure now, but everything depends on continued health.

Of course, sudden illness can strike anyone, and there is no insurance against it, but correct diet, regular exercise and avoidance of stress can minimise the risks. All people know that when they are below par even the most ordinary events can seem too much, and when they are on top of the world, the smallest pleasure is enhanced. Diet and

exercises have been examined in the preceding chapters. Stress is the next consideration. Determination is needed to stick to the diet and to do the exercises. Psychology can help.

First, you must want to train. However busy people are, they all make time for the things they really want to do. So list the reasons why you want to train. Health is clearly the first, but there are others. If you are a housewife and your figure has gone to pieces after years of domestic chores and child-bearing, then you will want to improve your looks. You can, by the methods already given. Follow them and you will be able to wear that bikini on the beach next summer. If you are a man with a middle-aged spread, butt of the office jokes ('his chest has slipped'), you can trim those inches away. Your looks, your attractiveness to your wife, even your sex life will benefit. In these days of mugging, older people are sometimes afraid to go out and may think wistfully of the time when they could have coped with muggers. Fitness will give you a better chance at any age, though of course it should not make you over-confident and reckless.

Another side effect of physical exercise is that it relieves anger and tension. Failure to come to terms with their own aggression is a cause of mental breakdown in patients. Hard, competitive sports can provide an outlet for anger and frustration. A few rounds of boxing in a club or a hard-fought game of squash are as satisfying in releasing emotion as striking the foreman or telling the boss what you think of him, and they are not so counter-productive.

Concentration on positive goals can prevent you brooding over ills. So much is wrong in the world and there seems so little anyone can do about it, that it is easy to despair, but it is futile to become depressed. Far better to channel frustration into some helpful activity, even if that activity is simply improving health and hence the ability to cope.

You must be convinced by now that you should train, so make it easy for yourself. Consider first, whether training at home or in a leisure centre would suit you best. It depends on your personality. Do you need the stimulation of others? Would the added luxuries of sauna, jacuzzi, beauty treatment, massage and refreshments that some gyms offer, help you to go on? Would the advice of a teacher or the discipline of a class make it easier to keep up? Would a training partner help you, and if so could you involve husband or wife or friend?

If you are strongly self-disciplined or would resent being told what to do, train at home, but in this case too, make it easy. Set aside a room. Keep the weights accessible. If you have to fetch them from the garage or the loft every time you will soon put off training on a busy night or when you are especially tired. It is no good promising to do twice as much next time, because if you did, you would over-strain yourself.

Training involves re-organisation of your life. Make a plan. People who say they cannot find time are always people who do not plan. The busiest people are often the very ones who will make time to take on some other activity. They can do so because they are organised.

Try putting down on paper your time-table for the day: when you get up, when you go to bed, mealtimes, working hours, travelling times. If you are a housewife, indicate the time spent cleaning, cooking, and when the children come home from school. Then, somewhere in that schedule, make a space for your weight training. The afternoon might be best for a woman in the home. The businessman might prefer the evening, or be able to visit a leisure centre in an extended lunch break, training before eating not after, of course. You can make time, if you really want to, and you will want to if you keep your motivation before you.

That motivation is unlikely to be the same as that of a young man or woman. Young people will aim at physical development, with or without the incentive of entering competitions. Older people will simply want fitness and health or to be slimmer and better looking.

If figure improvement is your aim, record all your measurements and weight as shown in the charts in Chapter 2. Measure them again at the end of each four-week period, and the improvement you see will encourage you to continue.

One lady was able to firm up her bust after breast feeding; another lost twenty-three inches around each thigh; one man added six inches to his expanded chest measurement after he had passed the age of thirty-five. It is never too late to make some improvement, though results come slower the older you get.

If slimming is your aim, prepare a graph, plotting weight along the upright and weeks along the bottom line. Weigh every week, and if you have followed the instructions in Chapter 12, you will certainly see the curve of the graph descend. If you are grossly overweight, have a photograph taken in your bathing suit. It will need courage, but when you compare it with the one you have taken six months later, it will all seem worthwhile.

There are a few other psychological tricks to help you make weight training a part of your way of life. First of all, make it fun. If you like music, do some of the rhythmic exercises to music. If you enjoy the sun, do your exercises in the garden in summer. Always train in comfort, whether at home or in a leisure centre.

Second, make the training sessions a habit. If you force yourself to train for three months, you will find it becomes progressively easier not to abandon them. We are all creatures of habit, and you can become hooked on training just as easily as on whisky or smoking.

The third trick is to reward yourself. The abstract idea of better health sometime in the future may not be enough. The promise of a new coat if you can keep it up for a month, or a holiday if you can keep it up for six months may well be the incentive you need.

Once you establish the habit of training, there is little doubt that the increased well-being you feel will provide sufficient motivation for you to continue. Remember that without health, riches, fame and success can never be fully enjoyed; with health, even disaster can be faced more confidently. The proper state for man or woman is a healthy mind in a healthy body. It needs only faith and effort to achieve both.

14 Coping with Stress

Everyone suffers a certain amount of stress, though it is probably only in the last two decades that people have talked about it or realised how much it affects their health. Formerly, people accepted stress and did not recognise it as a medical condition.

Stress places increased demands on the heart, blood vessels and other organs. It raises the pulse rate. If that stress is brought on by healthy physical activity such as playing a vigorous game, the pulse rate will quickly subside to normal when the game is over, and no harm will be done. If, however, the stress is related to a situation where we bottle up emotion, such as being reproved by the boss, then the rise and fall in the pulse rate is not so noticeable, and the bottled-up emotions can have an unhealthy effect on the body. Too many stressful situations in life can cause illness.

The parts of the body likely to be affected by cumulative stress are: the digestive tract, where it may show as gastritis, or stomach or duodenal ulcers; the skin, where outbreaks of eczema or psoriasis may occur; the heart, where angina or irregular rhythm may result; the mouth, where ulcers may occur; the lungs, particularly in asthmatic people, when stress can bring on an attack; the muscles, where nervous tics result; and the brain, where anxiety, depression, and, in severe cases, schizophrenia may result. Stress plays a part in the development of some forms of cancer, and the relief of stress forms one of the modern approaches to treatment of the disease.

Stress has many causes. For city people, pollution, rubbish in the streets, vandalism, noise, bright lights, the bombardment of advertising, high rise buildings, muggings, burglary, traffic hazards, the speed at which everything goes, including life itself, and the loneliness that the lack of a supportive community brings all cause stress. Country dwellers escape some of the ills of city life, but they can face loneliness and isolation, and may feel deprived of amusements, stylish shops, access to sporting and cultural facilities, and wider job opportunities.

Work is one of the prime causes of stress. Men may fear unemployment or being passed over for promotion. Women may not be given equal opportunities despite recent legislation. Both men and women may have to work under uncongenial supervisors and in unsatisfactory conditions. Staff may let them down, if they themselves are supervising. Poor pay and the resultant struggle to make ends meet, boring and repetitious tasks, complete lack of job satisfaction, and the struggle to keep up with other people all add to stress.

Housewives face stresses of their own. If tied to the house by young children, they may feel imprisoned, and resent not having money of their own. If they have all the latest labour-saving gadgets, they may be bored with too little to do; if they do not have them, they may envy neighbours who do. If they take a job to ease the money situation, they can easily become overworked, particularly if the husband does not help out with ordinary domestic duties.

Marriage can produce stress, particularly if there is fear or suspicion of unfaithfulness; if the husband is mean over money; if either partner is extravagant; if love has flown with the years; if there is a divergence of sexual needs. At thirty-five, both partners are nearing the menopause, which affects men as well as women, making both edgy, and increasing the tensions between them.

What is often not realised is that changes for the better make demands on us as well as changes for the worse. The Pools winner is often under more stress after he has claimed his fortune than when he was working at his familiar job.

People are very resilient. The body copes with a normal amount of stress and only when stress becomes cumulative and seems overwhelming, is it necessary to take action. Do you sleep badly? Does thinking about the future depress you? Do trivial inconveniences make you bad-tempered? Do you feel tired all the time? Do you find it hard to get on with people? Do you have difficulty in concentrating? If more than one of these conditions applies to you, then you may be carrying an unacceptable burden of stress.

Four things you can do: learn relaxation; practise meditation regularly; share your problems, and try to get a balanced view of life.

To relax, lie flat on the floor or on a firm mattress, wearing loose clothing. Put all worries completely out of your mind, and relax the body completely. Begin at the toes. Keeping your heels together, raise your heels and point your toes, so as to stretch the lower legs. Then lower them, relaxing the muscles and letting them drop like dead weights into the supporting ground or mattress. Lift your buttocks, thus stretching your spine, then lower. Stretch your arms and lift them just off the ground, before relaxing them and letting them lie like ropes by your sides. Consciously press your shoulders into the floor, then relax. Raise your head off the ground, and let it sink gently back. Now, try to feel that your whole body is limp, supported only by what you are lying on. Feel yourself sinking, with no tension at all.

Do this in a warm quiet room, and stay relaxed for five minutes, later increasing it to ten minutes. Do this daily, not only when you feel tense. With practice you will achieve a greater degree of relaxation. Let go all your worries.

In addition to this exercise, you will find that deep breathing will relax you if you have to face a stressful situation. Before that important interview or before being called to the dentist's chair, take a few deep breaths. It makes a difference.

If your worries lead to sleepless nights, you need to relax at bedtime. Do the above exercises, avoid a meal within three hours of bedtime, but have a milky drink. A short stroll before bedtime will help. Put your problems out of your mind as soon as the evening meal is over. Make sure the bedroom is cool but not cold. If you still cannot sleep, get up, and do some exercises to take your mind off your worries.

Meditation is the equivalent of relaxation on a mental or spiritual level. During the 1960s, 'transcendental meditation' was in vogue, due in part to the interest shown in it by The Beatles.

The aim of meditation, transcendental or otherwise, is to empty the mind of all distracting thought. To this end, teachers will give their pupils a 'mantra' to chant. A mantra is a word, often meaningless, on which to focus thoughts, so that all else is driven from the mind. You can pick your own word without going to a teacher. Repeat it silently to yourself, and if other thoughts come to mind, focus your attention on your word or mantra.

The whole idea is to banish thought by concentration on something that rouses no emotions in you. It need not be a word; it could be a picture. Religious people, in their meditation, turn their attention to God or to some aspect of holy living. It can be anything except the self.

Practise meditation for five minutes at a time, twice a day, and when you become more adept, lengthen the period to ten or fifteen minutes. If you like, you can combine it with your period of physical relaxation.

Bottling up emotions and problems has the worst effect. Like the safety valve on the steam engine, expressing emotions and problems helps release pressure. A good row to get things out of the system and allow a return to normal living is best, but if this release is not feasible, a sympathetic listener is the next best thing. By willingness to listen, spouses can help their partners in time of crisis. When overwhelmed by worry or anxiety, never to be too proud to seek for help. A doctor, a priest, a counsellor, even such organisations as Marriage Guidance

Bureaux or The Samaritans may be needed in severe cases. Often just talking things over helps because, by putting a situation into words, it becomes manageable.

Some things can be altered, some cannot. We need the wisdom to know the difference and the common sense to act appropriately.

Stress in work can be overcome by a change of employment, and if that stress makes you ill, it is worth making the change, even if it results in a lower living standard. This is an example of a case where something can be done. If action is possible, make up your mind and act quickly. Positive action is better than continual brooding and resentment.

Face problems one at a time. By allowing them to build into a mass of undifferentiated trouble, the tension is only increased. Treating each problem separately is like a man with several assailants who forces them to come at him one at a time.

Do not brood on your wrongs. Nursing a grudge will do you more harm than it does to the man who has wronged you. The Bible says: 'Let not the sun go down upon your wrath', and this is sound health advice as well as religious doctrine.

Try to see things in proportion, and to understand another's point of view. Missing an important meeting because your train is late may cause you to fume. Realise that it cannot be helped. The driver has not deliberately done this to you; indeed, he is probably worried himself, because he will have to explain why he was late to his superiors. Your delay is not worth more than a moment's irritation; if you carry the frustration into your meeting when you do arrive, it will colour decisions and achieve an importance out of all proportion to its significance.

A balanced view is helped by the inner calm that a religious or philosophical attitude can bring. It is helped too by balanced living. Do not be over-obsessed with one aspect of your life. There is a time for work and a time for play. Make that time, and you are far less likely to suffer from stress.

15 General Rules of Health

Apart from the things already considered – exercise, diet, avoidance of stress – there are a few other things that affect health, and these will be considered briefly in this chapter.

Hygiene The use of this word may have an emotive effect; we may retort that we are always clean; but hygiene means a lot more than washing hands and face and bathing regularly, or cleaning the teeth, important though these aspects are. It means storing food in covered containers, making sure pre-packed items are used by the 'sell-by' date, thawing out frozen food properly, cooking food thoroughly, keeping utensils scrupulously clean. It also means dressing sensibly in clothes that are comfortably warm and not restrictive, and in shoes that will not damage the feet. Older people can all grow a little careless in these matters.

Fresh air People can live without food for a couple of weeks, without water for a few days, but without air, we die in a few seconds. Pollution is one of the great dangers today. Some research suggests that lead in petrol results in city children having a lower IQ than those who breathe unpolluted air. Factory fumes, smoke, radiation are all dangerous to health, and it is essential to take every opportunity to breathe fresh air. Go to the seaside or into the country as often as you can. Sleep with the window open except in severe weather.

We breathe not only through our noses, but also through the pores, so we need to let the air get to the body, not only by wearing loose clothing, but by exposing the body to the air for at least some time each day. In summer, sunbathing and nudism are healthy pursuits; in winter even stripping to shower will give the body an airing.

Posture Bad posture is often developed unconsciously while sitting over a desk or bending over the kitchen sink. Without care bad posture will weaken the back muscles, compress the organs in the trunk, and affect breathing. It is easy to end up bent double. 'Stand upright, head up, shoulders back', used to be the command in the Army. The instruction is a recipe for health as well as for smartness. Good posture keeps us alert as well as young.

Try to keep your centre of gravity, which is a point just below the navel, inside a small circle drawn around your feet. You are then on balance. Stand upright, hands at sides. Do not lean forwards in the slouched position shown in Fig 71(a). Even if you use a stick to walk, when you become older, stay upright and do not lean forward to put your weight on the stick. Fig 71(b) shows correct posture.

Sleep Eight hours each for work, leisure and sleep is a good division of time. Some may manage on less sleep; indeed, need seems to diminish with increasing age, but it is not only the quantity of sleep but the quality that must be considered. The first five hours are usually deep sleep, the remainder a lighter state. Suggestions on getting to sleep were given in the last chapter, but if you have any regular difficulty, consult your doctor.

Minor ailments The older we get, the more important it becomes to look after ourselves. Minor ailments can quickly become major ones, and things that could be thrown

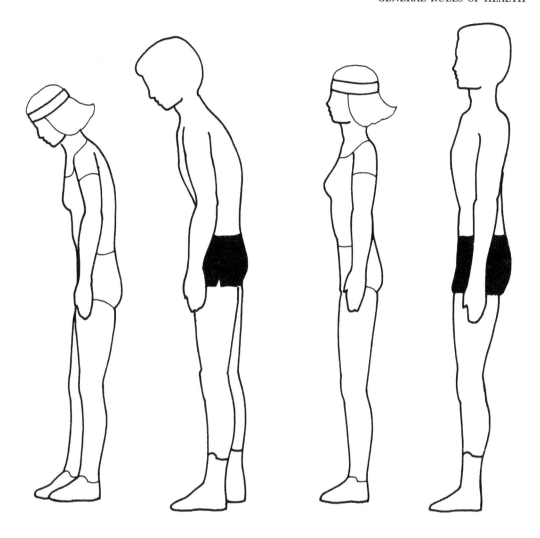

Fig 71(a) and (b)

off in the twenties become more serious in the thirties and forties. It is always sensible to seek medical advice early.

Some symptoms that should never be neglected are: rapid weight loss, high temperature, failure of cuts to heal, fainting spells, eye troubles, coughing up or spitting blood, shortness of breath, difficulty in urinating, any lump, particularly in the breast of a woman. These symptoms can indicate something quite minor, and no one should be unduly alarmed by them, but they might be serious and should never be ignored. Early treatment can often rectify matters.

Things to avoid Finally, there are some things so detrimental to health that it is common sense to avoid them at any age. They are:

Additives in food Colourings, preservatives and other additives pollute most convenience foods. Try to return to whole foods and organically-grown vegetables.

Constipation This leads to many worse conditions and should never be neglected. It is more widespread in civilised countries because of the removal of roughage from the diet. The best ways to fight it are regular exercise and the addition of bran to the diet.

Smoking The harmful effects of smoking

93

have been well documented, and research has shown that four out of five smokers would like to give up the habit. If you are one of these four, it is worth getting in touch with the local branch of Action on Smoking and Health (ASH).

There is a method you can try on your own however. First, identify the times when you do smoke. Is it after a meal, or when you are bored? Make a list of the danger times. Then list the benefits of giving up; set a date when you will give up. Announce it, so that pride will not let you fail. Stop smoking completely on that date.

You may need substitutes for the times when you used to light up. Try chewing gum or a sweet. You may find your hands empty. Twiddle a pencil. Avoid the situations, eg pub or club, where you formerly smoked, at least until the cure is complete. Use non-smoking compartments in trains and buses.

Finally, reward your efforts, by spending the money you formerly spent on cigarettes on some little treat, and as you enjoy it, remind yourself that it is only possible because of your savings.

Using these techniques, most smokers can lose the intense craving in eight weeks. The first four are the worst, so enlist the aid of family and friends in that early period.

Drinking Alcohol damages the brain and liver, and may affect the skin, heart and stomach. It may increase sexual desire, but it inhibits sexual performance. If you drink more than 2 pints of beer or 2 glasses of table wine daily, you are liable to damage your health. If you must drink, be moderate, but abstinence is considered even better by some people.

The danger times for drinkers are social occasions, with the pressure to conform. In pubs, everyone buys a round, and this leads to your having as many drinks as there are members of your group. At a party, you want to appear the generous host and you encourage your guests to partake freely by doing so yourself. Drink may lessen your inhibitions and make you feel more sociable.

Either give up altogether, which is not so 'way-out' as it would once have seemed, or set yourself a limit. When that limit is reached, if you are in company, change to non-alcoholic drinks; they are served in pubs and clubs these days. Three other tips are: do not drink alone; make each drink last a long time; dilute spirits.

It is worth noting that caffeine, the drug found in tea, coffee, and cocoa can also lead to sleeplessness, palpitations and other ills, if taken to excess. Keep your average consumption of these drinks to an absolute maximum five cups per day, but preferably substitute caffeine-free drinks such as fruit juice or beef or yeast extract.

Drugs It should be unnecessary to say anything about drugs, except 'Avoid them'.

Accidents The frequency of deaths from accidents comes just below those from circulatory and respiratory diseases and cancer, amongst older people, and the risk increases with age.

Do you follow all the safety precautions at work? Is your home well-lit and are exits kept clear? Do you take fire precautions? Is your electric wiring safe? Do you label medicines and keep them in a safe place? Do you throw away old ones? Are your stair carpets firmly fixed? Do you turn saucepan handles inwards on your cooker? Do you have non-slip mats in the bath or shower? When out at night, do you wear something light that will show up? Do you avoid drinking and driving, or driving when you are tired? Do you make sure your car is serviced regularly? Do you always look both ways when crossing the road?

These are only a few of the safety precautions you should be taking. Many of them were hammered into us when we were children, but as we grow older, it is easy to become careless. Be sensible, take plenty of exercise and you will greatly improve the quality of your life and sense of well-being.

Index